D0618571

*The Ultimate Home Business*
*Tax Reduction Strategy*

**Rhonda Johnson**          **Tom N Bass**

© 2012 by Encore Tax Inc. All rights reserved.

The text of this publication, or any part thereof, may not be reproduced in any manner whatsoever without written permission from Encore Tax Inc.

Tax: TheGame, Tax: TheGame...Let's Play to Win, and makingtaxagame.com are trademarks of Encore Tax Inc.

This publication is designed to provide accurate and authoritative information in regards to the subject matter covered. It is sold with the understanding that the publisher is not engaged in rendering legal, accounting or other professional service. If legal advice or other expert assistance is required, the services of a competent professional person should be sought.

Published by:

Encore Tax Inc.
3151 Airway Ave
Suite F109
Costa Mesa CA 92626

DirectSellersTaxExpert.com
PrePaidAuditSolutions.com
IgniteYourRecruiting.com
RhondaKJohnson.com

# Contents

# Foreword

You might think that building a home business could never be easy or fun. In fact, many of my clients are terrified when they even hear the word "taxes." My colleagues Rhonda Johnson and Tom Bass have done something amazing with their book *Making Tax a Game*. They have not only made taxes less intimidating, they have also offered extremely valuable tips that can save readers tons of money each and every year.

When you hire a random tax preparation company to handle your taxes, they just quickly do the return, charge you and then send you on your way. When you hire Rhonda and Tom to do your taxes, it is a process that ensures that each client gets the maximum deductions possible. They teach people about deductions that they never even thought were possible. That is why I love working with these guys and send them all of my referrals! Plus, they are licensed by the IRS and can prepare returns for all 50 states.

*Making Tax a Game* covers many of Rhonda and Tom's strategies. They back up all their ideas with concrete steps, guides, charts and useful and easy to understand plans, which are all geared towards helping the reader achieve tangible results. Of course, every step you take will leave you perfectly in line with the tax code.

Most people learn best when they have plenty of clear examples, and *Making Tax a Game* delivers on this front in spades. There are not just a couple of examples here and there so the authors can state that their book contains them. Instead the book provides well-reasoned and carefully thought out real world examples that all have a constructive aim, helping readers earn more and save more.

Additionally, *Making Tax a Game* contains practical tips that are surefire winners. These tips are designed to be pragmatic, making one's life easier and more organized come tax time. For example, one of the many helpful Tax Tips (and there are many placed throughout the book) is to take a large envelope along on your travels for the express purpose of collecting all travel related receipts, which can then be tagged based on their category. This is organizational genius at work! There is even a downloaded option for a "Trip Keeper" at the makingtaxagame.com website. Truly, this tip is just the tip of the iceberg. The makingtaxagame.com website also serves as a bona fide and substantial supplement to the book. It serves to increase the overall value of the book and is full of additional information and useful downloads.

If you are like many of my clients, you worry about dealing with the complexities of the tax system that relate to your home business. But after you read *Making Tax a Game*, you will find your fears start to subside. In fact, one of the key reasons why I recommend this book so much is the chapter "Build Audit Proof Support." This part alone *more* than justifies the purchase of this book!

Want to save money but avoid potential disasters down the road? Then take a deep breath and relax; this is your book! I find that many of my clients tend to get a bit panicky about how they are handling their deductions. By the end of the *Making Tax a Game*, readers will not only understand record-keeping, but also will have a firm grasp on how they can save tons of money through deductions, while still following all the rules. Rhonda and Tom understand the "tax game" and the audit experience inside and out.

I am calling *Making Tax a Game*, my final "step to success." This is the missing piece of the puzzle that everyone with a home based business needs to become a financially successful entrepreneur.

Belinda Ellsworth
Pinckney, Michigan

# Preface

# Use your home business to cut taxes and increase income

**TAXES—LARGEST EXPENSE**: The average American loses about 33% of their money to taxes, representing their single-largest family expense. Taxes alone cost the typical family more than their home, food, and clothes combined, and are, in fact, almost double the cost of any of the other typical family expenses.

Typically, the next biggest expense is only 17% for housing and household, about the same for automobiles, and only 12% for health and medical care. Your federal, state and local taxes represent not only your single-largest expense, but also the single largest source of potential savings for every American family.

**CASH FLOW—THE AMERICAN FAMILY'S BIGGEST CHALLENGE:**

The average American family now regularly finds itself with "more month left at the end of the money" instead of "more money left at the end of the month." It is no longer possible for most families to realize the quintessential "American Dream" of their own home, their own car, and a stable family due to the work and stress load they now find in the workplace, just trying to survive. The homes and cars they do own are mortgaged to the hilt, second mortgages are common, and they carry an average credit card debt load of over $6,000 at 18-21%; even if they sold all their assets, they could not cover the debt. They are insolvent.

In over 60% of all middle class families, either both parents work, or there is a single parent working. The children are being raised by day care centers, baby-sitters, and neighbors. When the parent(s) do arrive home, they are often too tired and too stressed to spend quality time with their children.

**THE ANSWER...** USE YOUR HOME BUSINESS TO CUT TAXES AND INCREASE INCOME.

# About The Authors

**Rhonda Johnson** is a uniquely qualified tax specialist. She is Managing Partner of Accountable Solutions...a full service accounting firm she started 20 years ago. Accountable Solutions has become one of the fastest growing firms serving direct sellers. She has 34 years of direct sales experience, over 20 years as a business owner and 9 years as a national speaker and author. As Director of the Prosperity Center for DSWA, the Direct Selling Women's Alliance, she has helped coach consultants in over 160 direct sales companies.

She has written four books including the best selling *Making Tax A Game.*

Captivating audiences with her enthusiasm...her well researched, high energy presentations are delivered in a down to earth style that reaches everyone. Featured as keynote speaker at numerous national events, Rhonda is an amazing tax educator!

She is dedicated to inspiring and motivating entrepreneurs to take control of their finances and feel valued for the profession they have chosen. Rhonda believes in paying your fair share of taxes...just not leaving a tip.

**Tom N Bass** with a degree in finance from Oklahoma State University, he spent the first twenty years of his career managing his family's home furnishings business. Under his direction, the operation grew from a single retail store into a regional chain. During that time he also developed a chain of delicatessens and a group of office furniture outlets.

His entrepreneurial spirit and extensive experience in start-up ventures and small business management and growth led him to continue his professional development into the arena of tax specialization. Tom passed the Enrolled Agents' exam at the top of his class, and is licensed in all fifty states by the

Federal government to represent taxpayers before the IRS in all administrative matters. As a result of his continuing education, he has qualified as a Fellow of the National Tax Practice Institute. Less than 1800 individuals have achieved this status. He is considered an expert in helping small business and home-based business owners maximize legitimate tax benefits and in turn, raise their profit margins.

In 1990, Tom teamed up with Rhonda Johnson to form Accountable Solutions, a unique accounting firm specializing in year-round client services for direct sellers. Through periodic contact, goal setting, performance analysis, and comprehensive tax evaluation, business owners are given the edge they need to win at the game of taxes, and keep more of what they make.

# Introduction

# Start a home-based business if you don't have one already

On a recent business trip to Seattle, Rhonda addressed a group of direct sellers. Most of these business owners were women. This isn't surprising, since 87% of direct sellers are women. On this particular occasion the attendees were asked to bring their spouses. Most of the men were assuming the "dream stealer" role and nudging their wives to go out and get a "real" job.

Rhonda realized she needed something to give these spouses to demonstrate the value of having a home-based business. She needed something tangible to put in their hands...something written that would dramatically show them why the direct sales occupation chosen by their wives would be enhanced by the available tax benefits. (Remember these are some of the same guys that won't ask directions.)

She decided to have Tom print a real tax return from their tax practice showing a husband and wife with two kids, living in California, owning their home, and both working W-2 jobs. Their combined income was $99,000. Then she decided to copy the return and make these simple changes:

1. She assumed the wife's $27,000 income was 1099 from direct sales.
2. She included expenses typical of a direct sales business.

The result was an additional federal refund of over $4,315 dollars. Not only did they get to keep an additional $4,315 of their money, they were able to save on many other types of expenses. Just look at all the other expenses that were reduced or eliminated:

1. No daily lunches out
2. No commuting mileage
3. Reduced clothing budget
4. Reduced or eliminated child care expense

She also wasn't working 40 hours, so there was more time with the kids. The savings in money were dramatic, but the extra family time was priceless. She also has an unlimited income potential. Additional tax savings are realized from the state and/or city taxes. Obviously, just like any other profession with a yearly income potential in excess of $100,000, learning and applying the skills and techniques of professional networking is critical to your success. As your income increases from your business, you need to align yourself with a professional home business tax preparation specialist. Our goal, however, is to INCREASE YOUR INCOME and therefore INCREASE YOUR INCOME TAXES.

**THREE STEP STRATEGY:**
Many people first look to their tax preparer to reduce their taxes, and they can help you do just that. But it is imperative to

understand that our goal, your goal, and the government's goal are all the same...we all want you to pay MORE taxes!

**Step One:** Cut taxes this year by converting current personal expenses to business expenses.
**Step Two:** Increase your total income by generating business PROFITS.

**Step Three:** Then, even with your new tax strategies, PAY MORE INCOME TAX!

Take advantage of the tax deductions Congress passed as an incentive for you to start and operate your business in order to generate business profits and increase your total income. This way, in spite of your new deductions, your total taxes go up!

For example, if you now pay $6,000 per year on $30,000 of income, we would all be pleased if you increased your income to $60,000 per year, even with the $10,000 in taxes you might owe. Your NET after-tax INCOME is now $50,000 instead of $24,000. The government is happy, we were happy to help you, and most of all, your family now enjoys a substantially higher standard of living.

**PROFIT MOTIVE:**
The quest for a profit through individual effort has long been a part of our culture.
Starting a home-based business affords you the opportunity to engage in this pursuit. Based on your profit motive, or intent to eventually obtain a profit from your business, you can enjoy

substantial tax advantages just like any other business. Your INTENT to obtain a profit from the operation of your home business provides he initial momentum for the road to success. While the term "intent" can relate to a number of facts and circumstances, your awareness of these factors can serve as a guide for the subsequent planning of business operations. The following factors, although not exclusive, are listed under the regulations of the Internal Revenue Code as relevant factors to be considered in determining if a profit motive exists in your business.

**Rule**: *You Must Have a Profit Motive.*

### Tests for A Real Business With a Profit Motive

**Test 1**. Has a Business Plan been prepared? (See sample in Strategy 6)

**Test 2.** What expertise does the owner (or do the advisors) have?

**Test 3.** How much time and effort will you apply to the business?

**Test 4.** Are you prepared to run the activity like a business?

**Test 5.** What is the income history?

**Test 6.** Will you keep adequate records?

**Test 7.** Are there elements of personal pleasure or recreation built in to your business?

**Myth:** *You Must Show a Profit*

Amazon.com lost money for over a decade, yet they wrote it all off. Logic dictates you wouldn't want to start a business and continually lose money, but if your business happens to lose money one year or more, you can deduct it.

For example, in 1982 a fisherman who had been in business for many years ceased business for health reasons. In 1988, after purchasing a boat, he again started tuna fishing. His 1990 Schedule C showed that he had caught and sold ONLY ONE FISH for the entire year, which generated an income of only $1,025 for that year.

Years 1991-1993 did not indicate the catch or sale of any fish at all. His expenses reported on his income tax returns during this time period exceeded $80,000. The IRS disallowed the taxpayer's losses under the rules relating to hobby losses. The Tax Court, however, saw it differently and ruled in favor of the taxpayer. The court said such factors as the prior experience and success of the taxpayer, his health (which included poor eyesight), and a relatively short fishing season (often less than twenty days per year) outweighed the negligible income obtained from the activity. The resulting NOL (net operating loss) can be carried back or forward to offset positive income.

# Two Tax Systems

Employees get to write off almost nothing, but businesses get to write off almost
everything. When Congress created the income tax in 1913, they set up two systems, one for employees and the second for employers. Since virtually all of the taxpayers were self-employed home-business owners (they were mostly farmers) at the time; the business tax system received preferential treatment. It hasn't changed since.

### Employees
Work Hard
Immediately Lose a Huge Chunk of those wages to taxes
Get to take home whatever is left after taxes are paid
Are entitled to limited deduction s

### Self-Employed Entrepreneurs
Earn Money
Spend for whatever they want or need
Pay taxes on whatever is left over
Are entitled to many deductions including
Mortgage Interest or Rent
Utilities such as Electric, Gas, Water, Trash
Cleaners to Dust, Vacuum, Empty Trash
Office Equipment...computers, copiers, telephones
Office Furniture...sofas, desks, chairs, tables, lamps
Supplies...paper, ink cartridges, stamps, staples
Décor...painting, pictures, rugs, carpet, wallpaper

Expenses...cell phones, iPads, iPods,

Subscriptions...magazines, books, online media

Travel...airline, hotel, meals, rental cars, tips

Acquiring clients...meals, sports tickets, entertainment

Security systems, cameras, guard dogs

Insurance...health, life, dental, vision, disability

Company Cars, boats, airplanes, trucks

Gifts...charity, 401k, SEP-IRA, profit sharing

Landscaping...gardeners, pool cleaners, snow removal

Holiday cards, postage, mailing service, flyer delivery

Marketing, advertising, promotion, social media, websites

Accounting, bookkeeping, legal fees,

Printing, copying, DBA filing, brochures, mailers, catalogs

> **Tax Tip:** If you have a home-based business operated with a profit motive, you can convert a portion of your personal, non-deductible expenses to deductible, business expenses.

## SUGGESTIONS TO VALIDATE YOUR PROFIT MOTIVE:

Maintain organized and complete business records. Utilize a separate credit card and checking account for business purposes. As necessary, secure registration, certification, business licenses, and insurance if required for your business. Utilize a home office and consider a separate business line. Regularly review your operations and make adjustments to improve the profitability of your business. Use a diary, calendar, and /or appointment book to keep track of your business activities. Our Receipt Tamer is ideally suited to help organize your receipts. **http://MakingTaxAGame.com**

## SET UP A PERSONAL INVOLVEMENT PLAN:

In addition to the customized business plan provided with this book, setting up a personal involvement (or daily activity) plan can simplify your actions as you proceed with the operations of your home-based business. Following such a plan will ensure that you qualify for maximum tax advantages, pursue maximum business profits (even on a very part-time basis), and substantially increase your income. Such a plan can include, but is not limited to, the following steps:

(1) **REVIEW** this manual thoroughly and plan your tax strategies accordingly. We recommend that you read this manual at least weekly for the first month after starting your business, and at least monthly through your first year in business.

(2) **PARTICIPATE** in any informational and training calls available for your specific business to both improve your knowledge and

facilitate your sharing of this information with your prospects and customers. Document these calls.

(3) **ORDER** supplies & materials needed to market the product, such as video and/or audio tapes, flyers, and magazine article reprints to distribute which promote your business;

(4) Assemble a LIST of potential customers for your new business.

(5) Set up a ROUTINE for your daily business actions. What days or hours will you dedicate to the operation and profit motive of your business?

(6) Set **TARGET BUSINESS TASKS** for you to complete daily. What do you want to accomplish and when?

(7) Keep a **DIARY**, calendar, and/or appointment book to keep track of your business activities. Follow up on uncompleted tasks or objectives.

(8) **MARKET YOUR BUSINESS**: Use the many available sales tools to market your new business services.

(9) Become a "**PRODUCT of the PRODUCT**" by implementing in your own family as many of the strategies outlined in this manual as are appropriate to your situation. Your tax savings and profit testimonial will be one of the most powerful business-building and profit-generating tools you could possible develop. The Result: By following the suggestions and overview of this intro-duction, you will start a process that will lead you through the three

steps of immediately cutting your taxes, increasing your income, and eventually being faced with increased taxes due to your increasing income. Now that's a problem we would all like to have, right?

(10) **KEEP MORE OF WHAT YOU EARN**: In order to keep more of what you earn, cutting taxes is the single most important money saving strategy you can employ for your family. Learning and applying the skills and techniques outlined in this book is important to your success, and to keeping your success instead of giving most of it to the government.

(11) **IMMEDIATE CASH BENEFITS**: Even before your first sale or earning your first bonus check from your home business, there are substantial immediate cash benefits available to you through tax deductions from your business.

Because you are starting your business with the intent to make a profit, your personalized Business Plan documents your legal right to convert the use of many of your former ordinary home expenses into substantial business tax deductions immediately.

Your home is now also your primary business location, and if your new business includes a broad spectrum of products, the business use percentage of your home and garage may qualify for beneficial tax deductions.

**HIRE YOUR CHILDREN:**
You can now hire your children between the ages of seven and seventeen to work for your business, and convert the former

25

expense of children's allowance to tax deductible wages without paying any payroll taxes. Now you may pay each of them up to approximately $5,950, TAX FREE to them and deductible to you, as wages for helping you in your business. For a family with 2-3 children, this deduction alone can be worth $8,800 to $13,200 in tax deductions, all because you are now in business for yourself, with your family!

**WRITE OFF YOUR HOME:**
Even the cost of your home itself becomes legally deductible through depreciation now available to you based on the business use percent of your home. In addition, most sole proprietors may take deductions of other home expenses, up to the extent of the net income of your home business, such as the use of your home while making product and sales presentations, sales meetings, sales trainings, communication, administration, or the display and inventory of products and samples used to generate sales and profits in your business.

Most home office deductions are based on the amount of space you use for regular business purposes, compared to the total amount of space in your home. This comparison, or ratio, is usually measured in either square feet or the number of rooms used exclusively for business purposes. Once you know the percent of your home you devote to your business, you can apply that same percent to your home's expenses, and determine how much of each expense is related to your business and, therefore, a potential tax deduction for your business.

## WRITE OFF YOUR CAR:

Your automobile, one of the most costly monthly expenses of the typical family,

instead becomes one of your largest tax deductions because you now also use it daily in your business.

## "FROM YOUR FRONT DOOR" DEDUCTIONS:

As outlined in your Business Plan, you may promote your business anywhere, every day. With a little planning and by properly documenting your use, a high percentage of the use of your personal vehicle can be deductible (see Strategy 2 for details). For a 20,000 mile per year business usage vehicle, this amounts to over $11,000 in tax deductions for your business each and every year, and even more if you use two vehicles in your new home business.

## SIMPLICITY:

Rather than a complex series of bookkeeping instructions, with confusing directions and exotic tax shelters, we recommend a system designed for simplicity and time savings for each new home-based business entrepreneur. Our recommended solution is either **The Expense Tracker** available at **http://IgniteYourFinances.com** or our **Making Tax A Game** software at **http://MakingTaxAGame.com**

# Strategy One

*"If you don't design your own life plan, chances are you'll fall into someone else's plan. And guess what they have planned for you? Not much."*

Jim Rohn

# Maximize your home business deductions

**HOME BUSINESS:**

Potentially thousands of dollars in tax deductions are available to any taxpayer that operates a business from his residence, which may be in a house, apartment, mobile home, condominium, or even a boat.

Generally, these deductions are available to the home-based business owner provided he uses the space regularly and exclusively for business purposes.

**OTHER STRUCTURES:**

You will also qualify for deductions on other structures on the property, such as a

barn, garage, greenhouse, studio, or other outside structure used for business purposes, such as an office or the displaying or storage of business inventory or samples.

**TEST:**

In order to qualify for the home business deductions, you must:

(1) Demonstrate your profit making intent (refer to your business plan and the guidelines in the Strategy 6 section of this manual)

(2) Regularly conduct your business from your home (bookkeeping, prospecting calls, conference calls, success line management)

In summary, you may qualify for your home business deductions when any dwelling unit of yours is used on a regular basis for your business.

> **Tax Tip:** *Opening a separate office location for your networking business or regularly conducting your networking business at a fixed location other than your home could jeopardize your home office deduction*

**MULTIPLE BUSINESSES:**

You may have more than one home-based business. Unrelated business activities are reported on separate Schedule C's. Two or more businesses may qualify for home office and other business deductions by allocating the qualified business use areas of the home to the appropriate business activity.

**EXAMPLE:**

You operate a second home-based business and may report each activity on separate Schedule C's. Both businesses could qualify for home business deductions, but must be determined separately. You may claim the business deductions for either or both of the qualifying businesses. (Ideally, you would allocate proportionate costs to each business individually.)

**PROPERTY EXPENSES USED IN YOUR HOME BUSINESS:**

(1) You may expense as accelerated depreciation newly purchased personal property obtained for exclusive use in your business

(2) You may expense as accelerated depreciation up to $133,000 of the cost of new business equipment (furniture, fixtures, computers,

etc.)purchased and placed in service during the same year that you used it more than 50% in your home business.

## CAUTION #1:

If you do not use the property or equipment exclusively for your home business, you may deduct only the business use portion of the property.

## CAUTION #2:

If you use the property or equipment for both personal and business use, you must maintain a usage log to validate the percent of business use or jeopardize your entire deduction.

## EXAMPLE #1:

You purchase a new computer for business use as well as family entertainment. You estimate business use at 90%. You may only expense 90% of the cost of the computer, and must maintain a usage log.

## EXAMPLE #2:

You also subscribe to cable TV, and use it to entertain the children of your visiting clients. You would probably not succeed in convincing the IRS that you never watch cable, so you may maintain a log of business usage, and expense the percent of business use. Below is a sample log.

| Date | Flat Screen HDTV | Biz Purpose | Time |
|------|------------------|-------------|------|
| 06/08/2012 | College Course | Mktg Education | 2hr |
| 07/21/2012 | Saddleback College | Training | 4 hr |

## EXAMPLE #3:

You purchase a new Wii game exclusively to entertain the children of your visiting clients. You may expense 100% of the cost of the Wii, and because it is 100% business use, you do not need to maintain a usage log.

## PROPERTY DEPRECIATION:

(1) If you convert personal property or equipment purchased in an earlier year to business use, you may depreciate that property, but it cannot be expensed.

## EXAMPLE:

You convert a two-year-old copier from personal to business use. You use it 95% for business. You may depreciate 95% of the lower of (1) its cost when purchased, or (2) its fair market value at the date of conversion.

## HOME BUSINESS DOCUMENTATION:

In order to verify business expenses, you need these, at a minimum, for each expense:

(1) A *receipt*; and (2) A *payment record*

You are free to determine your own method of record keeping for your home business, but you must keep records that document your home business deductions. You need invoices or receipts, proof of payment (checks or credit card statements), and any other evidence of paid expenses. Generally, you need to maintain these records for three years from the date the return was due or filed, or two years from the date the taxes were paid, whichever is later.

## DIVISION OF BUSINESS & PERSONAL USE OF THE HOME:

The expenses of operating your home are divided into personal and business use. Most networking home businesses use the cash method of accounting, where you deduct only the expenses you actually pay during the tax year; however, credit card purchases are deductible as of the date of the charge.

## BUSINESS PERCENTAGE:

In order to determine the percent of business use expenses you may deduct, you determine the relative area of your business usage in your home as compared to the area of your entire home by dividing the area of your business use by the total area of the home. You may measure the area in square feet.

## EXAMPLE:

Your home measures 1,800 square feet. You use three rooms that measure 720 square feet for administration, presentation, product display and storage for your business. Therefore, you use two-fifths (720/1,800), or 40% of the total area for business.

## DIRECT EXPENSES:

These expenses benefit only the business portion of your home, such as repairs, painting, and janitorial services for the rooms used in your home business. These direct expenses may be deducted in full.

## UNRELATED EXPENSES:

These expenses benefit only the personal portion of your home, such as repairs or painting your bedroom. These unrelated expenses are not deductible for your home business.

## INDIRECT EXPENSES:

These expenses occur as you typically run and operate your home. Indirect expenses benefit both your personal and business portions of your home, and include:

Real Estate Taxes

Deductible Mortgage Interest

Utilities & Services

Apartment or Home Rent

Home Owners or Renters Insurance

Repairs

Security Systems

Pool Service

Gardeners

Housekeepers

Casualty Losses

Depreciation on Your Home

General Maintenance

*You may deduct the business percentage of your indirect expenses.*

## ••• SPECIAL PLANNING NOTE:

As a Schedule C taxpayer with a qualified home business, you can save self-employment and Medicare taxes by moving many of the indirect expenses from your itemized Schedule A to your Schedule C to reduce the net income (and therefore self-employment and Medicare taxes) from your business.

### ••• DOUBLE DEDUCTIONS:

By converting many of your personal Schedule A deductions, such as mortgage interest, to deductions on your Schedule C, you still may take the standard deduction, which in effect may mean that you are happily enjoying "double" deductions.

### RENT vs. MORTGAGE:

When you rent your home or apartment (rather than lease or own), you deduct business rent based on the business use percentage deduction (BUP) of your home.

### MORTGAGE INTEREST:

You may deduct the business portion of your mortgage interest as a home business expense.

### REAL ESTATE TAXES:

You may deduct the business portion of your real estate taxes as a home business expense.

### UTILITIES AND OTHER OUTSIDE SERVICES:

Generally, the same BUP you realize on the home is used to compute the deduction you may take on your home electricity, gas, trash removal, cleaning services, etc.

### ••• SPECIAL PLANNING NOTE:

If you believe your utilities used for business exceed your normal business percentage, obtain evidence to support your assertion with a utility-use work sheet from your local utility.

## TELEPHONE:

The basic local telephone service charge, including taxes, for the first telephone line into your home is an unrelated and nondeductible expense.

## ••• SPECIAL PLANNING NOTE:

Your business-related long-distance phone calls on your first telephone line, as well as those on additional lines, are a deductible business expense. Also, any additional lines, cellular phones, pagers, fax lines, modem lines, etc. dedicated to business use are also deductible.

## REPAIRS:

The overall cost of repairs, including labor other than your own, that relates to your business is a deductible expense. For example, repair to the bathroom your customers would use benefits both the business and the home. Repairs are a necessary part of keeping your home and your home business in good working order for you and your customers. You may deduct the business percent of these common repairs, including: patching walls and floors; painting; wall coverings, window treatments, as well as repairs to roofs, gutters, sidewalks, or drives.

## SECURITY SYSTEM:

When you purchase, rent, or lease a security system to protect your home business, you may claim depreciation for the BUP of the security system along with deducting as an expense the BUP of the monthly expenses you incur to maintain and monitor the system.

## LAWN CARE:

While the IRS maintains in its publications that lawn care is an unrelated home expense and is not deductible, the U. S. Tax Court has found that you may deduct BUP of yard and pool maintenance costs. Therefore, the U.S. Tax Court has given you the authority to deduct the BUP of lawn care.

## CASUALTY LOSSES:

If you suffer a casualty loss on property used 100% for business, you may deduct 100% as a direct expense. If the loss is on property you use for both business and personal, only the BUP is a business deduction as an indirect expense.

## DEPRECIATION:

You may depreciate the cost of the building, excluding land (land is not depreciable), according to your business percent of use. Furnishings will also last more than one year, so previously owned furniture may be depreciated, while you may claim the expense election on new or used furniture purchased during the tax year according to your percent of business use for each item, provided that BUP exceeds 50%.

## PERMANENT IMPROVEMENTS:

Permanent improvements are those that increase the value of property, lengthen its life, or give the property a new or different use. A few examples of permanent improvements would be: updating electric wiring or plumbing, a new roof, a room addition for your home business, simple remodeling, or major modifications. Permanent improvements may be depreciated based on your BUP.

## ••• SPECIAL PLANNING NOTE:

You really should claim all applicable depreciation if you claim a home business. The IRS will compute your "basis" as if you did, regardless of whether you actually did or not, so by not claiming depreciation, you lose the benefit of the deductions, yet you still must pay tax on the profits just as if you HAD claimed the depreciation! Only in America!! (Actually, only in the U.S. Tax Code!!!)

> **Myth:** *Don't depreciate the home office portion of your residence*

> **Fact:** *The IRS will compute your "basis" as if you did, regardless of whether you actually did or not, so by not claiming depreciation, you lose the benefit of the deductions, yet you still must pay tax on the profits just as if you HAD claimed the depreciation.*
>
> Moral of the story? **CLAIM YOUR DEPRECIATION!**

# Strategy Two

*"We are continually faced with a series of great opportunities brilliantly disguised as insoluble problems."*

John W Gardner

# Maximize Your Business Vehicle deductions

**BUSINESS USE:**

Your automobile is a substantial expense, and therefore represents a substantial deduction to your business. If you use any vehicle in the course of operating your home business, that usage is deductible as a business expense. Because your vehicle will probably be used for personal use as well as business, you must maintain a usage log to validate business usage. You determine your deductions based on the business usage percent, which is the ratio of business usage miles compared to total usage miles.

**HOME BUSINESS RULING:**

In 1994, the IRS ruled that a trip from your home to a business stop is not deductible unless:

(1) Your home qualifies as your principal place of business, or your home contains a qualified home office, or

(2) You have an office downtown, or

(3) Your business stop was outside your metropolitan area and suburbs

Obviously, the importance of qualifying your home for the home business deduction as your regular workplace, and maintaining your product inventory and product samples becomes even more important, because with your home business qualification, you can then meet the guidelines of this IRS Ruling (#1 above) to take "from your front door" mileage deductions.

**COMMUTING:**
Driving directly from your home to a place of employment is a personal, non-deductible trip called a "commute."

**TWO BUSINESS LOCATION RULE:**
You may deduct as business mileage the miles driven between two business locations or places of employment or schools.

> **Tax Tip:** *Any time you leave after discharging duties at your home business and you make any business stop related to the home business, that trip becomes fully deductible. If you then continue to a secondary business stop (or place of employment), rather than considered a commute, that mileage becomes deductible under the two business location rule.*

**BUSINESS DEDUCTIONS:**
There are two methods to compute your annual mileage deductions: On Schedule C, you may annually deduct an amount equal to either:

(1)     The business standard mileage rate times the number of business miles traveled, commonly called "standard mileage deduction" (SMD), or

(2)  The actual costs of owning and operating the car multiplied by the business use percentage (depreciation or lease payments, maintenance and repairs, tires, gasoline, oil, auto club

dues, car wash & wax, insurance, registration fees, loan interest or lease costs multiplied by your BUP. You must maintain your usage log and keep all receipts and proof of payment to validate the business usage of your vehicle, regardless of which method you choose.

*Please note: Certain criteria apply to each method.*

### EASY MAXIMUM DEDUCTIONS:
Although some people will receive a more beneficial deduction using the "actual cost" method when computing auto deductions, the Standard Mileage Deduction (SMD) method is much simpler to track and compute.

### 2012 IRS STANDARD MILEAGE RATES:
55.5 cents per business mile
23.0 cents for medical or moving purposes
14.0 cents per mile driven in service of charitable organizations

### PLUS...PARKING & TOLLS:
Whether you choose the "actual costs" or "standard mileage" method of deductions, you may additionally deduct all business parking fees and tolls paid.

### INTEREST:
You may also deduct the business portion of any loan interest paid on your vehicle on your Schedule C, in addition to your license fees.

### EXAMPLE #1:

You lease a new $25,000 car for business use as well as family use. You log 20,000 business use miles, and 5,000 personal use miles this year for a business use of 80%. Using the standard mileage deduction, you would take an $11,100 mileage deduction (20,000 x $0.555) on your Schedule C.

### EXAMPLE #2:

Using the car from Example #1, you decide to use the actual cost method. Your lease payment is $550/month. You must track and total all receipts for gasoline, oil, insurance, registration fees, maintenance and repairs, tires, etc. You spent $2,000 on gas and oil; $1,000 for insurance; $500 in registration fees; and $200 for auto club, wash and wax costs. Because it is a new car, you only needed $300 for maintenance, and there were no repairs. Your total expense so far is $10,600, less a $70 lease inclusion cost. Your total actual expenses of $10,530 must be taken at your business use percent, which was 80%, so $10,530 x 80% = $8,424 deduction.

### EXAMPLE #3:

Use the car from Example #1, except that it was purchased rather than leased. You have the same expenses as Example# 2, except for lease payments. Instead, you are allowed to depreciate the car and deduct the interest you pay on the loan. For this example, the interest was $800. You must then compute depreciation based on luxury auto limitation rules. The scheduled amount for the year 2000 is $2,960. Your total expenses of $7,760 must be taken at your BUP, which was 80%, resulting in a total deduction of $6,208.

**Note:** The total amount deductible in Example #3 is even less than the amount allowed by taking the SMD in Example #1 for the same set of circumstances. Regardless of the method used, automobiles are "Listed Property" and are subject to special depreciation rules if qualified business use is 50% or less, or if your business use percent falls to 50% or less before the end of the recovery period (six years)

### ...WARNING...AVOID THE 50% RULE:

When you purchase a vehicle and depreciate it using the actual cost method, and if your business use drops to 50% or less, you must recompute the depreciation using the straight line method, then recapture the excess depreciation, which counts as **TAXABLE INCOME.**

### ...SPECIAL PLANNING NOTE:

If you use IRS standard mileage rates, your depreciation is built into the rate and is not affected by the 50% rule. This could be another great reason to use the simpler and easier SMD method.

### STANDARD MILEAGE RATE DEPRECIATION:

IRC 1016 requires that you use the standard mileage rate depreciation to calculate your car's adjusted basis (depreciated value). This is how you determine how much depreciation was included in the SMD. If using the SMD, you will need these figures to determine the value of your vehicle for tax purposes when you dispose of it.

The IRS SMD includes an allowance for depreciation equal to:

7 cents a mile for 1980 and 1981
7.5 cents a mile for 1982
8 cents a mile for 1983, 1984, and 1985
9 cents a mile for 1986
10 cents a mile for 1987
10.5 cents a mile for 1988
11 cents a mile for 1989, 1990, and 1991
11.5 cents a mile for 1992 and 1993
12 cents a mile for 1994 through 1999
14 cents a mile for 2000
19 cents a mile for 2008
21 cents a mile for 2009
23 cents a mile for 2012

In years before 1991, the IRS limited the standard mileage depreciation to the first 5,000 miles a year. Also, cents-per-mile depreciation rates will not apply to any year in which the actual cost method was used.

**NOTE:**
The basis of a vehicle may not be reduced below zero. Once the basis of a vehicle is depreciated to zero, the standard mileage rate continues at the same rate with none of the total allocated to depreciation.

## A SPECIAL WRITE-OFF FOR SPECIAL VEHICLES:

A few very popular large vehicles (such as a Chevy Suburban or Ford Excursion) carry lots of cargo, people, and **EXTRA TAX BENEFITS**!

These vehicles are large enough (GVW) to be excluded from the limitations to expense deductions imposed on most other vehicles by the luxury auto rules.

As business property, these "special" vehicles allow you to write off and deduct thousands more on your tax return in that same year, based on your BUP. See Strategy 1.

**Tax Tips:** *Audit-proof support for business auto expense*

## VEHICLE RECORDS:

Keep all records pertaining to the purchase, sale, and trade of any vehicles for at least three years after the tax year in which you dispose of the vehicle. You may need to document the basis (value) of a personal vehicle that you later convert to business use.

## Mileage:

Since your car is probably one of your largest monthly expenses, it's potentially the source of one of your most significant tax reduction strategies. If you use the same vehicle for both personal and business, the IRS requires that you maintain a log to determine what percentage of your driving is for business.

The record keeping takes no more time than it takes to fasten your seat belt. Simply keep a Mileage Log (available from www.makingtaxagame.com) in your car. Each time you turn on the ignition, you simply fill in four items:

| Date | Destination | Business Purpose | Odometer |
|------|-------------|------------------|----------|
| 06/08/2012 | Coffee Shop | Presentation | 23125 |

Destination and Business Purpose do not need to be precise. For example, under the heading Destination, you can simply fill in "Coffee Shop," and under Business Purpose, you can simply write "Presentation." Then just enter your odometer readings, or total miles traveled. [IRC Section § 274(d)]

> *Could it take more than 10 seconds?*

The IRS SMD includes an allowance for depreciation equal to:

10 cents a mile for 1987

10.5 cents a mile for 1988

11 cents a mile for 1989, 1990, and 1991

11.5 cents a mile for 1992 and 1993

12 cents a mile for 1994 through 1999

14 cents a mile for 2000

19 cents a mile for 2008

21 cents a mile for 2009

23 cents a mile for 2012

In years before 1991, the IRS limited the standard mileage depreciation to the first 15,000 miles a year. Also, cents-per-mile depreciation rates will not apply to any year in which the actual cost method was used.

## NOTE:

The basis of a vehicle may not be reduced below zero. Once the basis of a vehicle is depreciated to zero, the standard mileage rate continues at the same rate with none of the total allocated to depreciation.

### A SPECIAL WRITE-OFF FOR SPECIAL VEHICLES:

A few very popular large vehicles (such as a Chevy Suburban or Ford Excursion) carry lots of cargo, people, and EXTRA TAX BENEFITS!

These vehicles are large enough (GVW) to be excluded from the limitations to expense deductions imposed on most other vehicles by the luxury auto rules.

As business property, these "special" vehicles allow you to write off and deduct thousands more on your tax return in that same year, based on your BUP. See Strategy 1.

> **Tax Tips:** *Audit-proof support for business auto expense: The record keeping takes no more time than it takes to fasten your seat belt. Simply keep a Mileage Log (available from www.makingtaxagame.com) in your car. Each time you turn on the ignition, you simply fill in four items*

## VEHICLE RECORDS:

Keep all records pertaining to the purchase, sale, and trade of any vehicles for at least three years after the tax year in which you dispose of the vehicle. You may need to document the basis (value) of a personal vehicle that you later convert to business use.

## MILEAGE:

Since your car is probably one of your largest monthly expenses, it's potentially the source of one of your most significant tax reduction strategies. If you use the same vehicle for both personal and business, the IRS requires that you maintain a log to determine what percentage of your driving is for business.

A Seattle resident was in direct sales for many years. We asked to review returns numerous times. The response was always...no thanks our CPA is great, shouldn't be a problem. Years go by, more nagging to review. Client finally agreed to let us review the returns if there was no charge. After reviewing the returns we agreed to prepare the amended returns for the husband to review. If they decided to file we would get paid. The resulting amended returns yielded thousands in potential refunds.

Here's the rest of the story. CPA is next door neighbor, and been friends since preschool with husband. So he goes next door and asks his buddy to take a look and see what he thinks. Response was basically this new tax guy just shifted some stuff around and it looks good. So when ask the obvious question..why didn't you? The response was ... I don't do that type of accounting...I am a corporate guy and was just doing your returns to help out. You should probably let the new guy do your returns from now on.

# Strategy Three

*"Your income can grow only to the
extent you do".*

T. Harv Eker

# Maximize travel deductions

**GREAT ADVANTAGES:**
One of the greatest advantages of your home business is that you can make sales and build your sales team anywhere. That means whenever and wherever you go in pursuit of your business plan, your reasonable business expenses are deductible.

**COMBINED BUSINESS AND PERSONAL TRAVEL:**
We covered how to document your local transportation expenses in the last section, and this section will outline the parameters for maximizing your deductions when traveling for business purposes, even when combined with personal or family vacations.

**TRAVEL:**
The tax laws provide that you may deduct travel expenses you incur when your business activity requires you to sleep or rest away from your principal place of business with a home business, this means whenever you travel away from home.

**TEST:**
In order to meet the requirements for deductible travel and business expenses, your business activities on the trip must be:

(1) Appropriate and helpful to the development and maintenance of your business

(2) Conducted with the intent of obtaining a direct business benefit

(3) Customary and usual within your industry.

## BUSINESS DAY vs. TRANSPORTATION EXPENSES:

Expenses "on-the-road" are divided into two categories. When you pay airfare, vehicle expenses, etc. to transport yourself to an out-of-town business destination, you incur business transportation expenses. Once there, you may also incur business day expenses such as eating and hotel rooms. You may deduct food and lodging on business days, even when your trip does not include enough business days to make it a business trip

## THE 51/49% TRANSPORTATION RULE:

When you travel within the 50 United States (including Washington, D.C.) and spend more days (51% or more of your days) on business than you spend on personal time, you may deduct 100% of the cost of your transportation. However, if the purpose of the trip is not primarily for your business, you lose all of your transportation deduction for that trip.

## ...SPECIAL PLANNING NOTE:

Make sure that anytime you combine a business trip with personal or family days, that your primary purpose for the trip is business, and that you spend more days on business than personal pleasure.

## EXAMPLE #1:

You take a five-day trip from your home to Florida, but only work one day of the trip. You could deduct the food and lodging for the one day of work, but you could not deduct any transportation costs, or the cost of food and lodging for the other days.

## WEEKENDS, HOLIDAYS, AND STANDBY DAYS:

These days count as business days when they fall between business days during a business trip when it would not be practical to return home from your business destination over the weekend because of time required or expense involved.

## SPECIAL CONSIDERATION FOR SATURDAY NIGHT TRAVEL:

Airlines often offer large discounts if your flight days span Saturday night. If you can save on your airline ticket by staying over Saturday night you may count the stay-over days as business days.

## TRAVEL DAYS:

Travel days count as business days provided your point-to-point transit time plus business activity time for the day exceeds four hours. All out-of-pocket business expenses (including food) on travel days is 100% deductible.

## TRAVEL METHOD:

For business travel deduction purposes, it makes no difference whether you travel to and from a business destination by auto, airplane, train, boat, or bicycle. It doesn't matter if your car is large or small, if you fly first class, or if you charter a private plane; the transportation costs are deductible in full, with the exception of luxury boats (yachts or cruise ships), on which deductions are limited to twice the highest daily per diem rate allowed the executive branch of government for travel in the contiguous U.S.

**EXAMPLE #2:**

You plan a four-day, 300-mile driving trip to visit the home offices of your direct sales company for one day, and bring the family for a day of sightseeing. Your primary purpose is business, so your transportation costs, food and lodging are deductible. Food and lodging costs of family members do not qualify for deduction. If the hotel charges extra based on the number of people staying, simply deduct the base cost for one person.

**EXAMPLE #3:**

You attend your two-day home business convention with the family, driving four days to and from your home and the convention location. You also spend four days sightseeing. Your trip would still meet the 51/49% primary business rule, because you spent six of ten days on business. You would deduct 100% of the transportation and six days of food and lodging for yourself.

**CONVENTION/BUSINESS MEETING TRAVEL with SPOUSE:**

The tax laws give no deduction for travel of a spouse, dependent, or other individual accompanying the taxpayer on business travel unless:

1. The spouse, dependent, or other companion is your business employee, plus
2. For companions for a bona fide business purpose (be prepared prove this one); and,
3. The travel expenses of the spouse, dependent or other person would other otherwise be deductible.

The law makes it clear that your spouse not only must be an employee of your business, but also must travel for a bona fide business purpose. You get no travel deduction for the spouse's expenses when you bring your spouse to:

(a) Be the socially gracious spouse

(b) Staff the hospitality suite

(c) Be the assigned fraternizer

(d) Type notes, eat lunches and dinners

**ALSO NOTE:** The presence of your children at the travel site actually negates the business aspects of your spouse's travel.

### ...SPECIAL PLANNING NOTE:

If your spouse and children are employees of your business and they accompany you on the trip to do actual work for the business, then their travel expenses are deductible if yours are when you apply all of these rules.

### EXAMPLE #4:

You fly from home to California to build your sales organization, leaving Thursday, working Friday and Saturday morning, sightseeing through Sunday, working Monday, and returning home on Tuesday. All six days qualify as business days. You would deduct 100% of your transportation and deduct food and lodging for all six days.

### EXAMPLE #5:

The same trip as Example #4, but you vacation for four days at the end of the stay. The weekend is considered standby business days because you worked on Monday. You would again be able to deduct 100% of your transportation, as well as business costs for the six business days. You would not deduct food or lodging on the four final vacation days.

**EXAMPLE #6:**

The same trip as Example #4, but you leave on Wednesday, work Thursday, and stay over Friday and Saturday to save costs on airfare, and return home Sunday. You would deduct 100% of your transportation. You also would deduct your costs of food and lodging for each of the five days.

**RECOGNIZED TRAVEL EXPENSES:**

The following list of travel expenses are recognized as normal business expenses:

(1) Meals at 50% of cost, both en route and at the final work destination

(2) Lodging and transportation costs, including air, rail or bus fares, and the costs of transporting baggage, samples, or display materials

(3) The allocable portion of operating and maintenance expenses of vehicles

(4) Cleaning and laundry*

(5) Telephone

(6) Public stenographer costs

(7) Costs of transportation between an airport or station and hotel, from customer to customer, and from one place of business to another

(8) Tips incidental to the above expenses.

## * CLEANING AND LAUNDRY:

To be able to deduct the cost of cleaning your clothes, you must get the clothes dirty while in travel status (out of town overnight). You may get your travel clothes cleaned while out of town, or when you return.

> **Rule:** *This is only the first dry cleaning following a business trip out of town. Don't abuse this...it's not all of your dry cleaning.*

### "War Stories"

Two auditors show up to look at a local manufacturing business. The younger of the two had a noticeable "attitude". They had done some prior investigation and were sure we were cooking the books to hide taxable income in excess of $600,000. They didn't have a gold badge (Criminal Investigators have gold badges, handguns and always travel in pairs) so not to worry. After multiple visits amounting to 3 full days for two guys meticulously examining records they decided there was a technical violation. So we offered to accept their change which should allow us to make another change. They took 90 minute lunch to discuss. They came back and agreed to make both changes. The result was a $40,000 plus refund for the client over two years since their change for one year resulted in a loss we could carry forward and amend the following year's return.

Shortly thereafter the same client as above gets tagged for a Sales tax audit covering 3 years. After multiple visits examining the same records as the IRS the auditor indicates she will recommend no change. Subsequently she calls back and indicates she was overruled by her supervisor and needs more information. California is bankrupt and this is one of the plans to get cash...just squeeze, intimidate and bluff the business people to fork over cash they don't owe. Eventually the no change ruling was reinstated.

A caller from CT indicated his wife heard Rhonda speak at an event in Washington DC the previous year. It seems she had been in direct sales for only 2 years. He has been doing their returns on TurboTax. Unsure of all the deductions for direct sales he took his TurboTax return to a local CPA touted to know "direct sales". Apparently she was a former IRS agent. Six months has passed and no response from the CPA. We emailed back and forth...he has lots of questions, obviously above average intelligence. Finally told him, he has the worst possible combination to prepare the return. He should get his docs from the CPA, pay her, and send them to us. Subsequently we find out he has an MBA from Columbia and is the Controller for a Fortune 500 company. The return the CPA did was identical to the one he did on Turbo Tax. Ours resulted in an additional refund over $7,000 from the IRS plus the additional state refund over what he and the CPA had calculated.

# Strategy Four

*"Be thankful we're not getting all the
government we're paying for."*

Will Rogers

# Maximize your meals and entertainment deductions

**GREAT ADVANTAGES:**

Building your home business is not only easy, it's fun! You can save thousands, earn thousands, and cut thousands from your taxes through tax deductions for your home business. One of the big ones, and one which is often misunderstood, is the deduction for business meals and entertainment. Once you understand the rules, you can have fun while conducting your business meals and entertainment.

**IRS DEFINITION:**

For tax purposes, the term "entertainment" means any activity generally considered entertainment, amusement, or recreation, such as business socializing at theaters, country clubs, golf and athletic clubs, sporting events, night clubs, cocktail lounges, as well as trips for hunting, fishing, vacation, and similar trips, including such activity relating solely to the taxpayer or the taxpayer's family.

**DOCUMENTATION REQUIRED:**

For each individual item claimed under the business entertainment deduction, you must be prepared to document:

(1) The **AMOUNT** of each separate expense, although incidentals such as taxis, telephone, etc. may be simply totaled on a daily basis. The IRS allows you to prove amounts under $75 per transaction by

making an entry on your log or daily business calendar. For amounts $75 and over, you must have receipts to prove amounts spent. We suggest you save the receipts.

(2) The **DATE** of the entertainment expenditure or use of a facility for entertainment. For entertainment directly before or after a business discussion, record the date and duration of the business discussion.

(3) The **PLACE** of entertainment, with the name, address, or designation noted, along with the type of entertainment if not otherwise apparent; or the place where business discussion was held if entertainment is directly before or after a business discussion.

(4) The **PURPOSE**, or business reason, or business benefit to be gained or expected from the entertainment, along with the nature of the business discussion.

(5) The **RELATIONSHIP**, occupation, or other information relating to the person or persons entertained that shows their relationship to the taxpayer. Purchase the Receipt Tamer at our website to make this a simple part of your routine.

**TWO TESTS:**
You may deduct entertainment only if it meets either the:
(1) Directly related test, or
(2) Associated test

## DIRECTLY RELATED ENTERTAINMENT:

To be considered directly related entertainment, the expenditure must either (1) meet the four requirements test, or (2) occur in a clear business setting.

## FOUR REQUIREMENTS:

1. At the time you committed to spend the money, you had more than a general expectation of future business benefit.
2. During the entertainment, you actively discussed the topic that could produce future business benefit.
3. Your principal reason for the activity was the active conduct of your business.
4. You incurred the expense to speak with the person who produced your general expectation of future business benefit.

## CLEAR BUSINESS SETTING

You do not have to meet the four requirements above if you spent the money in a clear business setting. The clear business setting exception makes the entertainment automatically deductible as "directly related entertainment". Entertainment occurs in a clear business setting when:

(1) The person with whom you have the business discussion knows you are spending your money on the entertainment to directly further your business.
(2) You spend your money in a hospitality room at a convention where you display your products to further your business.
(3) You have no meaningful social or personal relationship with the people with whom you have the business discussion.

## BUSINESS SETTING:

You do not qualify for "directly related entertainment" when the entertainment takes place in a setting where you have little possibility of engaging in an active business discussion. Locations that make the business discussions unlikely include night clubs, theaters, sporting events, and cocktail parties. For directly related entertainment, the surroundings should be such that you have no substantial distractions to discussion. The IRS considers as conducive to a business discussion your home, a restaurant, hotel dining room, or similar place, not involving distracting influences, such as floor shows.

## ASSOCIATED ENTERTAINMENT:

If your entertainment is not directly related to the active conduct of your business, you may not deduct that entertainment unless:

(1) The entertainment is associated with the active conduct of your business, and

(2) The "associated entertainment" directly precedes or follows a substantial and bona fide business discussion.

Associated entertainment does not have to involve a business discussion. It takes place in a setting not conducive to a business discussion. To deduct associated entertainment, you must have a substantial and bona fide business discussion before or after the entertainment.

**Example:**

You know a prospective client would like to attend her town's professional football team's season opener; she's a huge fan. You email others in your company, and score two reasonably priced tickets for the game. Instead of inviting the prospect to go with you, however, you wisely let her know the two tickets are hers. She can ask whomever she wants. She's thrilled. With you!

When you arrange to give her the tickets for the next day's big game, you ask if she'll have a few minutes to share with you how she handles whatever it is you know your product can beat! She's so excited and grateful to receive the free tickets; she invites you in for coffee and to meet her equally excited husband. Soon, you have a new client eagerly touting your product.

You gained valuable face time with the prospect in a way few other people could, wrapped up a good piece of business, avoided the crowded game she was so pleased to attend, and went    shopping    with    your    girlfriends    instead.

You kept track of not only the cost of the tickets themselves, but your mileage to pick up the tickets, drive them to her house, and then return to your office or wherever your next business stop was for the day.

**BEST ADVICE:**

You should write down "why" you entertained someone after each entertainment expense. Relate your "why" directly to your business.

**50% RULE:**

Since 1994, tax laws limit your deduction for most entertainment and meals to only 50% of the otherwise deductible amount.

## NETWORKING OPPORTUNITY and/or TRAINING MEETINGS:

Expenses for networking business meetings which include actual sales presentations or training may not be subject to the 50% meals and entertainment rules, generally making them 100% deductible, because they are direct expenses of your business (even though the meeting might be entertaining depending on the speaker making the sales presentation).

This is true of any business, provided such expenses are reasonable in nature and directly benefit the business. Although a full meal is limited to a 50% deduction, there is an exception for the direct business expense of incidental refreshments, such as coffee, soft drinks, cookies, and appetizers. These expenses are fully deductible, and are treated the same as other business meeting costs, such as the hotel room rentals. You do not have to record "who, where, and why" for either opportunity or training meeting expenses, because the law exempts "directly related to business" meetings from the entertainment rules. The same exemption applies to business meetings of the taxpayer's employees, stockholders, agents, or directors.

**Tax Tip:** *You do not have to record "who, where, and why" for either opportunity or training meeting expenses, because the law exempts "directly related to business" meetings from the entertainment rules. The same exemption applies to business meetings of the taxpayer's employees, stockholders, agents, or directors.*

## "War Stories"

Southern California real estate agent. During the real estate boom he was consistently making 300k, and investing in rental properties in San Diego and Texas. When the bubble burst his income goes to virtually zero. After a year or so it rebounds to 50k or less per year. He lost his rental houses, his job, maxed his credit cards and was forced to borrow from friends to survive. We negotiated with the IRS and got him put on uncollectible status which means no payments and no active collections...even though he had $50,000 income

# Strategy Five

*"The reason most people never reach their goals is that they don't define them, or ever seriously consider them as believable or achievable. Winners can tell you where they are going, what they plan to do along the way, and who will be sharing the adventure with them."*

Denis Waitley

# Hire your children to realize BIG tax savings

**GREAT ADVANTAGES:**

This section is of great importance to those business owners who are parents. Your children generally work around the home anyway, so why doesn't your new home business actually hire them and pay real "tax-deductible" wages instead of "allowances" or "spending money" and, in this manner, allow both you and them to pocket the tax savings?

**THE LAW:**

The IRS recognizes that a child over the age of six may be a bona fide employee. The tax law specifies that wages paid by parents to children under the age of 18 are exempt from payroll taxes. The tax law also allows deductions for your ordinary and necessary business expenses, including wages paid to others for services they may provide to your business. Therefore, you may deduct wages paid when all of the following apply:

(1) The wages are reasonable in amount
(2) The wages are based on services actually rendered
(3) The wages are actually paid (by business check is best)
(4) All required federal and state payroll tax and W-2 forms are filed

## QUALIFICATION:

When you operate your business as a sole proprietor, you have an ideal tax planning opportunity by employing your children who are over age six and under age eighteen to work for your business.

## NOTE: OLDER CHILDREN:

Hiring your children over age eighteen still has advantages, even though they are no longer exempt from payroll taxes. If you are providing support or making any payments on their behalf (non-deductible), you can convert this amount into a business deduction by first paying wages to them for services provided to your business, then letting them use this money to make those payments themselves. If they are in a lower tax bracket than the owner/parent, this can save big $$.

> **Tax Tip:** *You will not be able to use this strategy if you incorporate your business, or have your business structured as a partnership, unless each partner is a parent of the child.*

## WAGES TO YOUR CHILDREN:

The IRS says you may deduct wages paid to your child when the facts show that your child:

(1) Did the work as a bona fide employee in the operation of your business and

(2) Received reasonable compensation for the work effort

The IRS has made it clear that a parent can employ his own child just as he could anyone else's child, and that it would not be rational to penalize the taxpayer who employs his child.

## EMPLOYMENT MUST BE BONA FIDE:

Your child's employment must be bona fide, and you must be able to prove it. The courts have stated that close scrutiny needs to be given when wage payments are made by a parent to their own child. Due to the family relationship, both a bonafide employer-employee relationship and an actual performance of services to the business must exist.

## BENEFITS:

You realize BIG potential tax advantages when you pay your child under age eighteen because:

(1) The wages paid will be tax deductible as a business expense; this reduces both income and self-employment tax.

(2) Both you and your children are exempt from Social Security and Medicare taxes on these wages. The total tax savings (combined percentages of these taxes) = 15.3% of the gross wages paid.

(3) Your children pay ZERO income tax on their earned income up to $5,950 in 2012, provided they have no more than $250 of unearned income (interest, dividends, etc.). This non-taxable amount changes annually, but is usually equal to the amount of the "standard deduction" for a single filer each tax year.

(4) Should your child's income exceed the non-taxable amount, only the excess is taxed, beginning at a rate of 10%. The actual tax rate is determined by the amount of taxable income. Also, as the child's tax rate

79

is most likely lower than the parent's, excess taxable income paid to the child results in another tax savings.

> **Tax Tip**: *State and local taxes typically follow federal rulings, but may vary depending on the state or local area. Contact your state Department of Revenue. For example, California does not require payroll reporting if the only employees are the spouse or children of the business owner.*

## FOOD AND LODGING ARE NOT CONSIDERED WAGES:

You cannot simply treat the value of the room and board you provide to your children as wages, no matter how bona fide the business relationship, because as a parent, you are legally responsible for providing such support to your dependent children.

## CHILDREN'S INCOME:

Your children may use the wages you pay them for whatever they like. It is their money. They can even contribute to their own support without endangering the parent's business deduction on their wages.

## EXAMPLE #1:

You earn $50,000 net after expenses, reported on Schedule C of your tax return, and live in a state with no income tax. You employed your three under age 18 children to answer phones, clean your office, and maintain your sample product inventory. They were each paid $4,000 for the year. You would deduct $12,000 from your net income on Schedule C, which would save you $5,196 in taxes

(28% federal income tax plus over 15% self-employment tax). Your children pay ZERO tax. The family is $5,196 ahead.

## EXAMPLE #2:

Same conditions as example #1, but as your home business grows, you earn $130,000 net. You pay your 17-year-old daughter almost $24,000 for her work, and the two younger children $4,000 each for their work for your business. Your daughter pays about $3,000 in taxes on her wages, and the other children pay ZERO. You save approx. $12,448 in taxes (36% Federal and 2.9% Medicare). Your family saves approx. $9,448 in taxes.

## PRIVATE SCHOOLS AND COLLEGE EDUCATIONS:

As another benefit of your home business, you may hire your children and allow them to pay for their own private school and/or college tuition (or even their weddings) with funds you previously would have paid to the government! By paying your children wages for services provided to your business, you secure the tax deduction for the business, and they may use the funds for whatever they wish, including paying their own private school or college tuition. By converting these former non-deductible personal expenses into business wage expenses, you realize a business deduction equal in amount to the tuition you formerly paid personally. Also, since your children probably enjoy a much lower tax rate than you, you'll also save a bunch on the taxes on the interest earned on these funds if deposited for college.

## ••• SPECIAL PLANNING NOTES:

(1) Use this strategy to pay wages to children who then use those funds to pay any of those "non-deductible" wants and needs that parents generally pay on an ongoing basis.

(2) Explore the many investment options available, such as IRAs, U.S.Savings Bonds, Series EE, etc. to gain even greater benefits. Many investments offer special considerations for higher education that qualify for tax deductible contributions for either tax free or tax deferred growth.

**EDUCATION ASSISTANCE BENEFIT:**

Up to $5,250 can be provided annually to qualified employees as a fringe benefit for qualified education expense; the amount is deductible as a business expense, and is "non-taxable" to the recipient.

**LIMITATION:**

A "qualified employee" does not include a spouse/employee, a dependent of the business owner, or the business owner's child under the age of 21. If any of these limitations exists, you may continue paying tax deductible wages as outlined earlier in this section.

**SUMMARY:**

When you hire your own children, not only do you get to work with someone you know, trust, and love, but you also get more business and more family benefit than you would realize by hiring an outsider. Here are four major advantages:

1) There are no Social Security or Medicare taxes on the wages you pay to your child under the age of eighteen.

2) There are no Federal or state unemployment taxes on the wages you pay your child under the age of 21.

3) You get the full value of the income tax deduction to your business, with the amount paid in wages being "totally tax free" or tax at a much lower rate.

4) The additional cash flow to the family expands in direct proportion to the tax savings realized.

**Lower Taxes = More Family Money Realized**

**CLEAR DOCUMENTATION REQUIRED:**

Should an audit occur, rest assured that the IRS auditors will question whether your children are really working for your business. They will generally look even closer at monetary transactions between you, your company, and your children than other regular business transactions. Therefore, you need to make sure that you follow the requirements and documentation of hiring your children just as you would any other employee.

**Here are seven easy steps that will provide excellent proof:**

(1) Register as an "Employer" with federal, state and local authorities

(2) Require and maintain all tax forms completed by the employee as required of an employer by Federal, state and local government. (such as W-4).

(3) Provide a brief description of the work to be performed by the employee (...will include but is not limited to ) and define the method and rate of compensation.

(4) Maintain a record of the results of the comparisons you have made to establish the rate of compensation, and note any other considerations you used as part of your basis for their compensation level

(5) Establish standard payroll procedures and follow the procedures closely, always paying by check from your company account

(6) Complete all required payroll forms and reports

(7) Apply your own common sense.

**EMPLOYER ID:**

When you employ your children, or anyone else, you must obtain a federal employer identification number (FEIN). This identification number will be assigned to you and will be used to report wages paid and to identify your payments of payroll tax. To register, complete federal form SS-4, Application for Employer Identification Number. This form along with instructions may be obtained by calling the IRS at 1-800-**TAX-FORM.**

Once you have completed this form, select one of the methods outlined in the instructions to complete the registration process. Once your FEIN has been assigned, proceed with and complete state and/or local registration (if applicable).

**TIME SHEETS:**

As in any business, you should require that time sheets be completed and turned in daily, weekly, or monthly by any employee, including your own children. With young er children, teaching them about and helping them complete time sheets daily is great preparation for their business future. This time sheet is actually your "receipt" as part of your record keeping that always requires a minimum of a receipt and payment record (your check) for each deduction taken.

Review the time sheet example below as a gui de for designing your own. Please note that the time sheet documents the date, task, and time spent working.

| Month _____ | | Child's Name _____ | |
|---|---|---|---|
| Day of Week | Date | Description of Tasks Performed | Hours Worked |
| _____ | ___ | _____ | |
| _____ | ___ | _____ | |
| _____ | ___ | _____ | |
| _____ | ___ | _____ | |
| _____ | ___ | _____ | |
| _____ | ___ | _____ | |
| Total Hours Worked | | | _____ |
| x Hourly Rate | | | _____ |
| Total Wages Paid With Check _____ | | | |

> **Tax Tip**: *The IRS will disallow your payroll deduction if you can't prove your kids actually worked for the money you paid them.*

## DOCUMENT COMPARABLE WAGES:

You have the burden to document that the wage you pay your child is comparable to what you would have to pay any third-party employee or worker to do the same type of work.

## NOTE:

We recommend calculating the compensation for all family members, regardless of age, by applying an hourly rate to the hours worked rather than by using salaries.

Using an hourly rate method and daily time sheets automatically accommodates the record keeping of the detail of specific hours worked, which is a factor in maintaining audit-proof support in several areas.

## EXAMPLE #3:

You pay your daughter $8.00 per hour to prepare mail packets for your prospects. She prepares 20 packets per hour. You tried using one of your neighbors who only produced 25 packets at $10.00 per hour. The wage level for your daughter appears comparable, and can be documented by keeping records on both workers. Have your neighbor sign the time sheet when paid, and make sure the description includes the number of packets made for both. The time sheet combined with your summary constitutes very convincing evidence.

**EXAMPLE #4:**

You define the work to be performed and also define any requirements you may have. For example, you may need someone who is flexible and can work any shift, seven days a week. (Even the IRS has pay considerations for working evenings and weekend shifts.) Submit your criteria to the various job placement services in your area and document the quotes you obtain of the hourly rates for the services and requirements you have outlined. You can then use this comparison to determine the hourly rate you will pay your children while also documenting that the wage level is comparable for your area.

**COMMON SENSE SUMMARY:**

A great common sense method for building support of the wage level for your child can be generated by answering the following questions: "What work does my child do for the business?" and "Why am I paying my child this amount?" Answer those two questions in writing and file your answer with your other business tax records.

**ALWAYS PAY BY CHECK:**

Whether your employee is your minor child or any other worker, always pay wages by check. This will establish a clear paper trail from your business checkbook to your child's bank accounts, while creating a clear business image, and training your child to regularly add to his savings.

> **Tax Tip:** *In 2012 you can pay each of your kids from age seven through seventeen $5,950 tax free to them and tax deductible to you.*

**EMPLOYEE RECORDS:**

As an employer, you are required to obtain and maintain certain records for each and every employee, even if your only employees are a child and/or spouse. Each employee file should contain:

(1) Federal Form W-4: Employee's Withholding Allowance Certificate. Your employee (including spouse or child) will use this form to tell you how many exemptions and allowances he or she claims

(2) State Form W-4: (if applicable)

(3) Federal Form 1-9: Employment Eligibility Verification

(4) Description of work to be performed

(5) Results of market comparisons or other considerations (particularly when employing family members)

(6) Date of Employment, compensation plan

(7) Copy of any reimbursement or fringe benefit plan(s) that are applicable

**NOTE:**

You are required to keep these records even when using a payroll service.

## PAYROLL RECORDS:

As an employer, you are also required to maintain records of the hours worked, the wages paid, and taxes withheld (if any) for all employees, even if the only employees are family members. This information will be used to generate the required reports throughout the year, including providing each employee with a W-2 at the end of the year. Since the paperwork is not hard to complete, you could even hire your child to complete it as one of his responsibilities as an employee of your business. Talk about great business training! Or, you may choose to use a payroll service provider. This service will normally include the preparation of all required government payroll reports. Accountable Solutions provides this service for a nominal fee. Any amounts spent for this service are tax deductible; therefore, your actual out-of-pocket cost is reduced by the amount of your taxes saved. In addition, this time saved can be reinvested in building your business, expanding your profits, quality time with your family, recreation, or almost anything more interesting and profitable than paperwork.

## MINIMUM AGE:

The IRS has approved the hiring of your child over age six. Although you may have younger children that actually help you in your business, can you justify, or do you want to try to justify, using a four-year-old to answer the phone? Can he take a message for you and write it down? For your own peace of mind, you will probably want to stay with the "over age six" guidelines as your minimum age.

## CHILD LABOR LAWS:

If you hire your own child to work in your home at tasks that do not involve heavy machinery, dangerous chemicals, driving cars, etc., you and your child are probably exempt from child labor laws. To be sure, call the labor department in your state for a definitive answer, and make note of the person's name, title, department, and the date of your conversation for your files.

Accountable Solutions Family Payroll Service:

A 100% IRS compliant, turn-key payroll
service is available for a nominal fee at
http://makingtaxagame.com

"War Stories"

Direct sales diva from Seattle. 10+ years in direct sales. Sure her preparer was doing a good job. After nagging her for 3 years finally got to look at the most recent returns. Amended three years and got additional refund of over 10,000.

Same scenario in Bay area. Husband been doing returns on TurboTax. Prepared amended returns for three years (that is the most you can amend). Additional refund for all three years exceeded $25,000.

# Do you qualify for a Family Payroll?

Is the family member working for a trade or business that is a corporation, an estate, or a partnership where only one parent is a partner, or a partnership where one spouse is a partner?

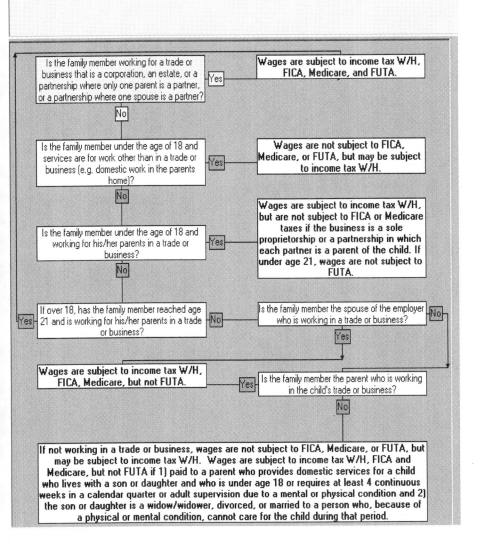

91

# Strategy Six

*"Try not to become a man of success
but rather to become a man of
value."*

Albert Einstein

# Business deductions you never knew you could take...

## *Over $25,000 in deductions available for each child employed in your business!*

Here's how:

- Take the kids OFF your personal return. They won't be dependents.
- Each child will file their own tax return.
- Each child will setup an IRA and deposit up to $5,000 annually.
- You, as the employer can pay each child under 18 up to $9,750 totally free from Social Security taxes, Medicare taxes, Federal Unemployment taxes, or Federal income taxes.
- Your business can now put up to $11,500 in deferred compensation, as a SIMPLE retirement account contribution, into the IRA of each child. Plus, the business can match up to 3% of the employee/child's contribution (an additional $345) into each IRA as its contribution to the SIMPLE plan.
- The business can pay up to $5,250 in expenses (subject to additional age restrictions) for any kind of education. This payment is excluded from the gross income of the employee/child.

- Each employee/child can use the money in their IRA (both amounts contributed from wages, and the amounts deposited as part of the SIMPLE retirement plan) to pay for higher education without being subject to the 10% early withdrawal penalty that normally applies to IRA withdrawals before the IRA owner reaches age 59½.

## RESULT

Your business has deducted over $25,000 and NO TAX IS DUE on any of it. In the 28% tax bracket, you have just saved over $7,000! And each of your children has a significant college fund and/or an IRA that could be worth over a MILLION dollars when they are ready to retire.

> **Tax Tip:** *Has your tax preparer told you about any of these deductions?*
> *This is just a sample of the innovative tax-saving strategies we exhaustively research exclusively for our clients.*

Do you have children ages seven to seventeen? List their names and ages....

_____

_____

_____

_____

_____

_____

What jobs could they perform for your business that you would consider paying someone outside the family to do?

List the jobs:

_____

_____

_____

_____

_____

_____

_____

_____

*Generally, anyone with children can take advantage of one of the greatest tax saving opportunities granted by Congress. This tax benefit was established to both encourage home businesses with tax free earnings, and also encourage saving for higher education using tax deferred earnings with Educational Individual Retirement Accounts.*

*For each child employed in the family business, you are entitled to deduct approximately $5,950 annually, tax free, for each child. Just the savings in federal taxes alone approaches $2,000 for each child. (Visit our website for more details: www.makingtaxagame.com Click on SERVICES, then HIRING FAMILY.*

## "War Stories"

Direct seller in Phoenix heard us on a teleconference. She called later and told us they were being audited for three years and the bill was $25,000 plus. After we got the documents, her husband had already gone through the first step of the audit. After talking with the auditor...he had a PHD and was definitely above average for the IRS, we discovered the husband, a school teacher, had been doing their returns on TurboTax for years. This was the first returns with her new direct sales venture. She hit the top of the pay plan the first year. Basically he had followed the TurboTax wizards and managed to enter the mortgage interest and other items 3 times. The resulting refunds were thousands more than they were entitled to receive. This dramatically illustrates why you need to know something about tax before you start the engine. Call from PA. Husband wife team selling sensual lotions and scented candles. Not so unusual except they are Amish and selling to church members. Same story, much bigger refund than local CPA. Amended returns to boot.

# Employment Agreement

As of_____ (date), _____(name of employer) agrees to employ _____ (name of employee) to perform duties as specified below, subject to change from time to time as mutually agreed in writing, and subject to curtailment at any time at the employee's sole discretion.

1.  **Duties shall include:**

     a. _____

     b. _____

     c. _____

     d. _____

     e. _____

     f. _____

     g. _____

     h. _____

2.  **Term.** This agreement shall begin on the effective date specified above and shall continue until terminated by

3.  **Compensation.** Pay shall be weekly, biweekly, monthly

$ _____ per hour, upon submission of completed timesheets, with a maximum of _____ hours per pay period specified above.

4. **Additional Compensation.** If work is offered, agreed to, and performed outside of the scope specified in Para. 1, or as

amended, additional remuneration shall be as mutually agreed by both parties.

5. **Expenses.** The employee is expected to promote the employer's business as a part of his or her ongoing dudes, and thus may incur expenses from time to time for entertainment, meals, travel, club dues, etc. All such expenditures, if
pre-approved by employer, will be reimbursed within 30 days of submission of Claim for Reimbursement of Employee Incurred Business Expenses, along with required receipts and/or documentation.

6. **Vacation.** The employee shall be entitled to take _____ days vacation per year, during which time compensation will/will not be paid.

7. **Disability.** If employee is unable to perform his/her duties for a period of two consecutive weeks due to illness or incapacity, his/her compensation will continue at a rate 25% less than full compensation, period of up to six months. Vacation will continue to accrue during this absence. Upon return to full employment, full compensation will be reinstated.

8. **Employment at Will.** This is an employment at will agreement, meaning that the employer has the right to terminate this agreement at any time for any reason, or for no reason, upon giving the employee at least two (2) weeks written notice.

9. **Severance Clause.** If termination is for any reason other than for cause, two weeks compensation shall be provided on the final day of employment, as a severance fee.

10. **Entire Agreement.** This document, plus any attached and cosigned Addenda, shall serve as the entire agreement between the two parties.


**AGREED AND ACCEPTED:**

| | |
|---|---|
| _____ | _____ |
| EMPLOYER | EMPLOYEE |
| _____ | _____ |
| DATE | DATE |


> **Note:** *This may seem like a harshly worded agreement for your family, but it is another step to qualify your Family Payroll as a deductible business expense.*

## "War Stories"

Direct seller making 40 to 50k per month for several years. She is married with two kids. Generously gives away much of the money...making house payments, etc for others. Within a matter of months she moves into a million dollar house, gets divorced, and her mlm goes out of business overnight. Didn't save anything...owes the IRS eventually 170k...hadn't filed any returns for 5 years. It took several more years to get everything filed and deal with IRS collections. Eventually she was put on uncollectible status by IRS which means no active collection activity.

WA resident making money in various MLM companies for years. They hadn't filed returns for the previous five years. Husband was an athletic coach at a local community college. His withholdings would have yielded sizeable refunds if they had just filed every year. She fears doing something wrong on the returns and creating problems with the IRS so she does nothing. Not sure what is deductible, etc. Mind frick.

IRS will only issue refund checks for previous three years. Failing to file means leaving cash on the table by procrastinating. We called her one day, and left a message on voice mail asking if we could show her how to get $10,000 in the next 20 minutes would she would call back. She did. Then we asked her to just throw everything related to her business and taxes into a box and get on a plane to Orange County. She spent three days in our office on the floor sorting paper. Still didn't have enough to file...but could see big bucks coming back eventually. It took another year to get enough to file...finally talked husband into getting the missing documents. The result was in excess of $17,000 refunded for the most current three years. They forfeited more than that to the IRS by not filing sooner.

Call from VA. Husband in law enforcement. Has "drug sniffing" dog at home and works at the Pentagon. His wife had been doing the returns on Turbo Tax. Turns out she is now the MLM star and in her previous incarnation was a beta testing software bug finder/fixer guru for an accounting software company. The most anal retentive person I ever talked to. Anyway her added refund over her version in the 7-8 thousand range.

# Strategy Seven

*"Designing your product for monetization first and people second will probably leave you with neither."*

Tara Hunt

# Build audit ready support

**OVERVIEW:**

Three of the greatest fears in the United States are public speaking, death, and an IRS audit. Many people would rank the fear of the IRS as #1! In reality, most fears are based on a lack of knowledge and confidence. Now, we can't do anything today about the first two, but you do not need to fear the IRS if you follow the rules.

**LEGAL BUSINESS:**

The first thing you can absolutely believe in is your legal right in the United States to own and operate your own business, your legal right to enjoy the profits of that business, and your legal right to take every legal tax deduction available to your business.

**PROOF OF PROFIT MOTIVE:**

Proving that you are actually in business with the intent to make a profit is easy due to your customized business plan. Simply follow your business plan, and the guidance we provide and be sure to document your regular business-building activity. Use a separate (personal) credit card and checking account for your business.

## AUDIT PROBABILITY:

The odds of your return being audited are very low, with less than 1% of individual returns ever audited. Even if your return is selected for audit, you have nothing to fear if you build adequate documented support for the deductions you claim. When your deductions are reported and documented properly, you can expect to see a "NO CHANGE" stamped on your return, if you are ever audited.

## TAKE EVERY LEGAL DEDUCTION:

The IRS is charged with collecting every penny the law requires you to pay: but according to those very same laws, you are legally entitled to use those laws and the "Taxpayer's Bill of Rights" to assure that you take every legal deduction allowed by those same laws in order to save every possible penny!

## IT'S UP TO YOU:

Your accountant does not "take care" of your taxes, any more than a dentist takes care of your teeth. Both of them attempt to help you "clean and repair" those things you did not take care of, after damage is done. Most tax services and accountants simply fill in the blanks on your return to report the information you give them. It is up to you to decide what you will document and give to them.

## "THE BOOKS":

The traditional "books" (Balance Sheets and Profit & Loss Statements) are kept by most businesses. As most independent contractors in networking operate their home business as a sole proprietor, they are not required to keep Balance Sheets. However, you will need to prepare a summary of your income and expenses, generally called a "Profit and Loss" or P&L summary, and be prepared to document that summary.

## THE BIG THREE:

The IRS divides business activity into three separate categories. You should align your business tax planning and documentation into these three areas as well. By following the path of the IRS, you can structure your accounting and record-keeping to accommodate an audit. This will save you time and money when preparing for an audit. These are the "big three":

(1) **Income** (2) **Expenses** (3) **Proof of Payment**

**INCOME:** All money deposited into your bank accounts will be considered income unless clearly identified and provable as non-income. In addition, the IRS conducts cash flow analyses on individuals (income vs. expenses) to look for additional income that may not have been deposited or reported.

## EXPENSES:

Individual bills, invoices, receipts, time sheets, usage logs, and credit card slips are needed to support business expenses.

## PROOF OF PAYMENT:

Method of payment on all expenses listed above is needed to prove payment of business expenses to be deductible.

Individual refills printer cartridges at home. 150k plus income. Uses 100% of garage, 2 outbuildings, and 2 bedrooms in the house for storage, office, production. In business for years. Existing CPA not giving any home office deduction. Amended past three years returns. Got an audit notice. Someone reviews all amended returns and selects a small sample to audit. Went to audit with box of receipts. Talked to auditor about his John Wayne pictures and fighter plane pictures on the wall. I am a pilot and fan of the "Duke". Convinced him that we had reviewed the bookkeeping in QuickBooks (basically done his work for him). We never opened the box to look at any of the documentation. Just showed him the totals by category of what was originally submitted and then compared that to what we could prove. He accepted everything we suggested even an overlooked deduction of 12,000 on one year. We walked out with the IRS having to write the client a check. End of story...client got refund initially in excess of $7,000 plus the added money at audit. Do you think they were pleased? No, wife (dream stealer) decided it was our "fault" they got audited so they fired us. Go figure. Probably $10,000 ahead but the emotional impact of the audit made it "bad". This was my first official audit.

# Six Files

| File 1 ***Advertising/ Promotion*** | File 2 / ***Office Supplies*** |
|---|---|
| Paid advertising, mailing list fees, leads, CDs, DVDs, networking, direct mail postage, flyers, team incentives, brochures, website, SEO, catalogs | Stationery, pens, business cards, copy paper, toner cartridges, file folders, phone systems, envelopes, janitorial, computers,cellphones, iPads, printers, fax, file cabinets |
| File 3 / ***Home Business*** | File 4 / ***Office Business*** |
| Rent, mortgage payments, utilities, property tax, gardeners, home owners insurance, housekeepers, Cuban pool boys, alarm systems, pest control, repairs, maintenance, improvements | Business license, credit card statements, interest, bank fees, postage, delivery, dues, subscriptions, internet access, tax prep, rent legal fees, bookkeeping outsourced, utilities, medical, payroll |
| File 5/ ***Travel / Entertainment*** | File 6 / ***Vehicle*** |
| Airfare, hotels, meals, taxis, rental cars, entertainment tickets, tips, your Trip Keepers | Mileage Log, gas, parking, repairs, DMV, lease payments, purchase interest, insurance, |

# Take care of the big three!

**DAILY DIARY - APPOINTMENT BOOK:**

There is no question that a daily appointment book or computerized contact manager will help you organize yourself for greater sales and business efficiency, while your usage log on your vehicle or other "dual use" equipment (like your video camera, if used for business as well as personal use) will document the daily activity in which you engage that generates business expenses. Your phone bill documents your outgoing long distance calls from within your home. Appointment books are not required documentation for tax purposes, but in many prior audit cases they have served as the best prima facie evidence of profit-motivated business activity. A thoroughly documented daily business calendar listing the details ("who, what, when, and where") of business activity is your best defense in the event of an audit.

**THINK LIKE AN AUDITOR:**

An auditor is paid to find discrepancies. Do not fear this; simply make your records audit-proof. Examples of discrepancies:

- Hotel receipts that show double occupancy on business trips that were expensed at 100% (You would then have to prove deductibility on the  spouse)
- Airline tickets that show additional stops on the itinerary on a business trip (Side trips might indicate non-deductible sightseeing)
- Credit card slips with children's or spouse's signature could indicate their use of a business vehicle.

- Overstated mileage on vehicle usage log when those numbers don't match mileage and dates noted on periodic service and/or repair bills

## KEEP IT CLEAN:

As the owner of a qualified home business, you are entitled to many deductions not available to the typical wage earner. There is no need to "pad" your expenses. Simply provide proper documentation of the "Big Three" and concentrate your real efforts on increasing the growth of your business and income.

## BURDEN OF PROOF:

The taxpayer has the burden of proof as to what items are qualified tax deductions. However, the taxpayer is the one who defines what he has, and the IRS is forced to prove otherwise. If the taxpayer does not define his own deductions, then the IRS will define them to its best advantage and leave it up to the taxpayer to prove otherwise. In other words, if you don't define what you have they will! It's up to you!

## IN THE EVENT OF AN AUDIT NOTICE:

First of all, don't panic. Just like an auto accident, it would be unfortunate if it ever happened to you, but relax and call your tax preparer. If you are contacted via telephone concerning an audit, give only the minimal and basic information required. Never discuss the accident (audit), nor offer apology or accept blame. In the event of an audit, get professional representation to appear for you. NEVER go to an audit yourself! If you are ever notified of an audit, immediately contact your tax preparer.

**Example:** You receive an audit notice from the IRS, so you wisely contact your tax preparer immediately. She reminds you to remain calm and that all your documentation and paperwork are in order.

When the IRS auditors arrive, they announce they're looking for more than $600,000 in taxable income they believe you're hiding! On numerous visits totaling three full days, two auditors meticulously examine your records and eventually decide there was a technical violation. You and your tax preparer discuss this, and tell the IRS auditors you'll accept their change which opens the door to you and your tax preparer making another change. The IRS auditors return after lunch, during which they discussed your offer. They agree to make both changes—theirs and yours. The result: you get a $40,000 tax refund! The IRS's single change resulted in a loss on one year's tax returns, which you and your tax preparer then carry forward to the next year. By amending that year's tax return, you secure the $40,000 refund.

# The Pursuit of Business Profits

*Income:* Business revenue. Active and passive remunerations for goods or services sold through business activity. Does not include loans to the business.

*Expenses:* Ordinary and necessary business spending consistent with the profit purpose of the business.
*Sample Expense Categories*

*Advertising:* Team incentives, brochures, ads, business cards, website, stationery

*Banks:* fees, credit card fees, interest

*Cars & Trucks:* Business mileage, tolls, parking, DMV, interest or actual expenses instead of mileage may be used

*Commission & Fees:* sales commission, referral fees, city business license

*Employee Benefits:* health insurance, child care, company car, profit sharing

*Insurance:* liability, E&O, vehicles
*Legal & Professional:* tax preparation, bookkeeping, audit protection, legal

**Home Office:** A percent of all residence related expense

**Rent or Lease:** Office, storage, equipment

**Repairs:** Equipment, building

**Supplies:** Office, shipping, marketing, postage, shipping, shop, warehouse

**Taxes & Licenses:** payroll taxes, sales tax, business license

**Travel:** airlines, meals, lodging

**Meals & Entertainment:** business meals, sports tickets, concerts,

**Utilities:** Cell phones, cable, DSL, internet, website

**Wages:** Payroll records in separate binder

**Cost of Goods Sold:** Items purchased for resale

**Equipment:** Purchased or transferred from personal to be used in the business and depreciated.

**Loans:** Personal funds invested in the business that you can pay back to yourself tax free.

**Owner's Draw:** Nondeductible profit taken by the owner.

# Financial Statements

Financial Statements are an accountant's daily newspaper. They tell him/her what is happening, both big and small, good and bad, with your business. Financial Statements include income and expense reports, balance sheets, cash flow projections, comparisons and many more.

The following financial statement is a simple income and expense report which is typically prepared monthly, quarterly and annually. This is one of the easiest to use and most important for income tax reporting. What about you? It's your business and I know you want to track its success. It shouldn't take more than an hour for each quarter to do the job.

*Isn't it worth four hours and fifteen minutes of your year to know how successful you have been?*

Here's your schedule:

**April:** Total each expense file folder for January, February, March...plus your total business income for each of these same three months. List these totals on the statement and do the final calculations to see how much money you made this quarter.

**July:** Totals for April, May and June

**October:** Totals for July, August, September

**January:** Totals for October, November, December

**January:** Total the previous four quarters for the annual report

# Profit Summary – 1<sup>st</sup> Qtr

| INCOME | 1<sup>ST</sup> MTH | 2<sup>ND</sup> MTH | 3<sup>RD</sup> MTH | TOTAL |
|---|---|---|---|---|
| ADVERTISING | | | | |
| OFFICE SUPPLIES | | | | |
| HOME BUSINESS | | | | |
| OFFICE BUSINESS | | | | |
| TRAVEL ENTERTAINMENT | | | | |
| VEHICLE | | | | |
| | | | | |
| | | | | |
| TOTALS | | | | |

# Profit Summary – 2nd Qtr

| INCOME | 1<sup>ST</sup> MTH | 2<sup>ND</sup> MTH | 3<sup>RD</sup> MTH | TOTAL |
|---|---|---|---|---|
| ADVERTISING | | | | |
| OFFICE SUPPLIES | | | | |
| HOME BUSINESS | | | | |
| OFFICE BUSINESS | | | | |
| TRAVEL ENTERTAINMENT | | | | |
| VEHICLE | | | | |
| | | | | |
| | | | | |
| TOTALS | | | | |

# Profit Summary – 3rd QTr

| INCOME | 1ST MTH | 2ND MTH | 3RD MTH | TOTAL |
|---|---|---|---|---|
| ADVERTISING | | | | |
| OFFICE SUPPLIES | | | | |
| HOME BUSINESS | | | | |
| OFFICE BUSINESS | | | | |
| TRAVEL ENTERTAINMENT | | | | |
| VEHICLE | | | | |
| | | | | |
| | | | | |
| TOTALS | | | | |

# Profit Summary – 4th Qtr

| INCOME | 1ST MTH | 2ND MTH | 3RD MTH | TOTAL |
|---|---|---|---|---|
| ADVERTISING | | | | |
| OFFICE SUPPLIES | | | | |
| HOME BUSINESS | | | | |
| OFFICE BUSINESS | | | | |
| TRAVEL ENTERTAINMENT | | | | |
| VEHICLE | | | | |
| | | | | |
| | | | | |
| TOTALS | | | | |

# Profit Summary – Annual

| INCOME | 1ST MTH | 2ND MTH | 3RD MTH | TOTAL |
|---|---|---|---|---|
| ADVERTISING | | | | |
| OFFICE SUPPLIES | | | | |
| HOME BUSINESS | | | | |
| OFFICE BUSINESS | | | | |
| TRAVEL ENTERTAINMENT | | | | |
| VEHICLE | | | | |
| | | | | |
| | | | | |
| TOTALS | | | | |

This Business Plan Template is provided to you
by Accountable Solutions

accountable solutions
THE DIRECT SELLERS' TAX EXPERT.

# IGNITE YOUR FINANCES
Business Plan for Home Based Business Owners

BUSINESS PLAN OF: _____

DATE ESTABLISHED: _____

Business Plan

# Table of Contents

## Business Plan of:

A sole-proprietorship business

## Vision Statement

My company, _____,
founded on_____ as a home based business, intends to profitably mass market a growing number of products and services to the general buying public. Due to low product prices, high retail profit margins, large target audiences, and the tax incentives available to me by running this as a home-based business, I intend to produce a substantial profit over a period of time.

## Mission Statement

My company,_____ , will provide high quality products and services at the best prices to my customers through personal sales, direct marketing, paid and or non-paid advertising, home based product demonstrations, catalog sales, online promotion, fundraising support, etc.

## Target Market Prospects

The target market prospects for my company's products and services fall into these general market categories:

1._____
2._____
3._____
4._____
5._____

## Customer Profile

The ideal prospective customer possesses these qualities and or needs:

1. _____
2. _____
3. _____
4. _____
5. _____

## Competitive Environment

1. Our competitor_____ which provides _____

2. Our competitor_____ whose product line includes_____

3. Our competitor_____ whose market advantage is _____

## Our Marketing Advantage

In order to successfully sell against our competitors we intend to market in the manner of

_____
_____
_____
_____
_____
_____
_____
_____
_____

# Our Marketing Plan

Our company_____will develop and deploy a marketing strategy that will aggressively promote_____ premier products and services on a nationwide and international basis through retails customers, friends, relatives, business associates, and prospects generated through direct mail, websites, and other direct marketing activities capitalizing on the fact that we offer these three distinct benefits:

1._____

2._____

3._____

My daily plan as CEO of our company_____
will be to promote the business starting with a prospecting list or sales call as my first stop upon leaving my primary business location (home) every day, continuing as possible throughout the day. Each evening, prior to returning to my primary business location, I will make a final prospecting call. This will include but not limited to:

- Prospecting and making price comparisons at various merchant establishments rather than simply "shopping".
- Prospecting and promoting my company's products and services whenever playing golf, fishing or any other social or sporting activities conducive to business discussions.
- Promoting my company's products and services at church, school, and numerous other appropriate activities.

# Sales Strategies

We will capitalize on the unique sales advantages of our products and services by employing the following strategies:

- *Direct Sales:* Many of my retail customers with entrepreneurial potential will be converted to product distributors by simply showing them the advantages of owning their own business and how they can save by buying products at wholesale prices for personal use as well as profit from retail sales to their customer base.

- *Gift Giving:* Once recipients of gift certificates contact me for redemption, I will offer them the opportunity to convert to an Independent Marketing Associate or Distributor status in order to enjoy lower product costs for personal consumption.

- *Fundraising:* I will provide FREE membership in my organization to any Non-Profit Organization in order to help them establish, promote and conduct a successful fundraising program. As a member, the organization may order products at wholesale and sell at retail. One unique program for fundraising groups is to order gift certificates at 50% off retail and then sell them to the group at 25% discount

- *Networkers:* It's estimated that 17 million Americans are involved in Network Marketing today. My company provides a high quality product and service at a competitive price point giving my business substantial advantage in the market; therefore these millions of networkers are prime candidates for my opportunity.

- **Direct Mail:** In order to reach these networkers and millions of people interested in starting a business, buying my products and services, I will conduct an aggressive direct mail campaign as part of my marketing efforts.

- **Classified Ads:** We will explore the use of classified ads to reach our target market.

- **Word of Mouth:** We will offer incentives to our existing customers to provide references for additional prospects.

- **In-Home Meetings:** Home presentations are planned to showcase all of our exciting products and services in order to reach a large group of prospects that know us on a first name basis.

- **Internet:** We intend to aggressively utilize the internet to present our message and showcase our products and services.

## Conclusion

Our company_____will establish a track record of cost-effective products, excellent support and exemplary service to our customers. The products and services offered by _____will continue to expand and diversify as we move forward.

Following and initial period of startup losses,_____ intends to grow business top line and bottom line revenue and reaching profitability in the shortest timeline possible. Our company_____
_____ intends to become a premier, exceptionally profitable tax-paying business entity.

128

# Want Your Tax Return Audit Ready?

## *Keep Good Records!*

The primary reason folks leave money on the table is due to lack of good record keeping. That's right: they are overpaying their taxes by thousands of dollars simply because they don't know what deductions are available. If you don't know how to track the deductions you are aware of, you are leaving the IRS a big tip! You need to treat your business like a business, so it will pay you like a business! Here's the minimal amount you need to do:

1. Separate your business and personal income and expenses.

    a.    Get a separate personal checking account for your business.

    b.    Use a separate personal credit card for business.

    c.    Carry both your personal and business checks and credit cards with you all the time.

    d.    When you make a purchase, decide right then whether it's business or personal and pay with the appropriate check or credit card.

    e.    Avoid cash transactions. Keep the receipts if you must spend cash.

2. Cash Payments: Receipts / Invoices / Statements

    a.    File them by month.

    b.  Sort them into one of just six categories

    c.  Enter the totals

3. Checks

    a.  Reconcile the bank statement.

    b.  Your deposits should equal your business income.

    c.  Don't count transfers from personal accounts

    d.  Don't count credit card advances.

    e.  File statements by month.

    f.  Divide the checks into one of six categories.

    g.  Enter the total

4. Credit Card Statements

    a.  Code each item into one of six categories.

    b.  Total each category.

    c.  Enter the total.

*We recommend you avoid cash transaction unless there is no alternative.*

# Strategy Eight

*"We have too many people who live without working, and we have altogether too many people who work without living."*

Charles Reynolds Brown

# Limited health insurance Deductions when self-employed

**GREAT ADVANTAGES:**

As a self-employed business owner, you are entitled to deduct a percentage of your health insurance premiums as an adjustment to income. As this lowers your adjusted gross income (AGI), greater benefit may be realized for other deductions that are subject to limitations based on a percentage of your AGI.

**QUALIFICATION:**

The self-employed deduction applies to health insurance premium costs paid by the sole proprietor to cover himself, his spouse, and his dependents. You may deduct the cost of commercial insurance. Qualified long-term care insurance contracts will generally be treated as accident and health insurance contracts for the purposes of the self-employed health insurance deduction.

**LIMITS ON THIS DEDUCTION:**

The tax law limits the amount of this deduction to the net profit from the business activity (Schedule C) minus the deductions for one-half of self employment tax, Keogh, SEP, and SIMPLE contributions. It also does not have the advantage of reducing self-employment tax as does Strategy 8.

## LIMITS WHEN ELIGIBLE FOR OTHER COVERAGE:

During any month that the self-employed individual is eligible to participate in any subsidized health plan maintained by either his employer or his spouse's employer, the self-employed health insurance may not be claimed.

## ••• SPECIAL PLANNING NOTE • UNLIMITING THE LIMITS:

Employers may deduct 100% of the cost of medical insurance and 100% of the cost of medical reimbursements provided to all employees under a qualified medical reimbursement plan. Even if you are eligible to participate in a subsidized health plan maintained by an employer, you are often personally responsible or the deductible (often $500- $1,000 per family member annually) and the co-pay percentage of 20% or more of major hospital bills. Either way, if married, study Strategy 8 of this manual to learn how to employ your spouse in your home business and start a 100% medical reimbursement contract as an employee fringe benefit. It must cover ALL employees, but when your spouse is the ONLY employee, and coverage is extended to cover his children (your children), and his spouse (you) as part of the contract, you may be able to enjoy 100% deductibility on all family medical expenditures.

# Strategy Nine

*"Your attitude, not your aptitude,
will determine you altitude."*

Zig Ziglar

# Hire your spouse or child for more medical benefits

**GREAT ADVANTAGES:**
Because the self-employed health deduction applies only to health insurance, and also limits the deduction, you might get far greater benefit by hiring your spouse to work for your home business. By hiring your spouse, you can pay 100% of the medical expenses of your employee (your spouse) and your employee's dependents, including yourself.

Even if your spouse has other health coverage, there are generally deductible and co-insurance features in addition to other non-covered items that your business could pay through a qualified medical reimbursement plan. Then, you can deduct the medical expenses as business expenses on your Schedule C, again lowering your AGI and income taxes as well as your self-employment tax.

**EXAMPLE #1:** Assume that you operate your Schedule C business and employ your spouse with wages of $10,000 per year. You could adopt a written employer-provided accident and health plan covering all of your employees. If during the year you reimbursed your employee (your spouse and family) for $5,000 in medical expenses not covered by insurance that would be a deductible business expense, along with the spouse's wages and the family medical coverage. A business owner/parent could also employ one or more of their children and enjoy a 100% medical reimbursement plan for the children's medical expenses.

••• **CAUTION:** This deduction is only valid if the spouse is a bona fide employee. You must report the spouse as an employee, maintain all payroll records, and pay payroll taxes just as you would for any other employee as required by tax laws. Realize that other related businesses could be affected as well.

**WRITTEN MEDICAL REIMBURSEMENT PLAN:** Although the law does not require that your medical plan be in writing, it does require that plan benefits are an enforceable right of the employee. Therefore you need your plan to be in writing. The plan should commit the business to certain rules for payment and be provided to all employees as a definite policy well before someone gets hurt or sick.

**DISCRIMINATION:** Laws concerning equal treatment of all employees in medical plans (as well as other areas) are enacted and amended regularly, so you will want to get professional assistance in setting up your plan to avoid inadvertently violating regulations.

**SPOUSE WAGE STRATEGY:** As a Schedule C taxpayer, you do not pay unemployment taxes on wages paid to your spouse. However, both your business and your employee pay Social Security and Medicare (payroll) taxes on the employee's wages. Therefore, the lower the wage, the lower the payroll taxes. A minimum wage paid to your spouse would still allow this reimbursement plan, but you will pay less payroll tax.

# Self-Insured Medical Reimbursement Plan

Effective (date), (your company name) hereby establishes the following Health and Accident Reimbursement Plan for the exclusive benefit of its employees. This Plan is to be considered "Secondary Coverage" for those employees who are covered under any other Medical Insurance Plan or Plans.

1. **Reimbursement for Medical Expenses**

   a. As of date of employment, per Employment Contract, all employees of _____, whether employed full-time or part-time, qualify to be reimbursed for all Medical Care expenses incurred by the employee and not eligible for coverage under any other Insurance Plan(s) in effect at the time the cost(s) was/were incurred. This Plan is to be considered Secondary Coverage, for reimbursement only.

   b. For purposes of this Plan, Medical Expenses shall be defined by IRS Code, Section 213(d).

   c. This Plan also covers any employee's spouse and the employee's legal dependents, as defined in IRS Code, Section 152.

   d. For minor employees, defined as employees less than 18 years of age, any and all benefits due under this Plan will be made payable to the parent or legal guardian of the employee.

e. In lieu of providing reimbursement for expenses for which the employee or his/her dependent would be eligible under this Plan, the employer may, at his/her option, elect to pay the expenses directly to the service provider.

f. Benefits under this Plan shall be limited to $     per eligible person per Plan Year.

2. **Continuation of Compensation During Periods of Disability.**

a. Short Term Disability. Effective immediately upon employment, should an employee covered under this Plan become disabled and unable to perform his/her duties as specified in his/her Employment Agreement, his/her Compensation will continue at a rate of 25% less than full Compensation, for a period of up to six months.

b. Long Term Disability. If disability continues for more than six months, employer shall, beginning in the seventh month, pay the employee at a rate of 50% of his/her normal full Compensation, until the Employee is able to return to work, or for one year, whichever comes first.

3. **Secondary Coverage**

a. As previously stated and alluded to, eligibility for reimbursement under this Plan shall be limited to such amounts as not covered under any other Medical Insurance Plan under which the employee/dependent is covered and/or any government Medical Reimbursement Plan under which the employee/dependent is covered.

## 4. Covered Medical Expenses

   **a.** In addition to costs customarily considered to be "medical expenses", this Plan also included costs for annual eye exams, reading glasses, contact lenses and /or surgery to correct vision, routine dental check-ups, and any and all necessary and required dental preventive care, repair and restoration, and outpatient or inpatient treatment for chemical dependency, drug/alcohol abuse and psychiatric disorders.

## 5. Termination and Amendments to this Plan.

   **a.** The employer may, at his/her sole discretion, elect to terminate or modify this Plan for any reason.

   **b.** Any termination of this Plan or changes or modifications thereto shall be communicated to all covered employees in writing at least sixty (60) days prior to the effective date of the termination or change in coverage.

## 6. IRS Exclusions

   **a.** It is the intent of the provider of this Medical Coverage that all medical benefits paid to any eligible employee under this Plan shall be eligible for exclusion from the gross income of the employee and/or his/her parent or legal guardian, as provided for in Sections 105 and 106 of the Internal Revenue Code.

**Employee Acknowledgement:**

I have read this employee benefit entitled Self-Insured Medical Reimbursement Plan and I understand how it applies to me personally.

_____

Employee

_____

Date

_____

Employee Printed Name

# Strategy Ten

*"A goal without a plan is just a wish."*

Antoine de Saint-Exupery

# Paying estimated taxes

Any individual who is self-employed, retired, laid-off, or disabled, knows or should know they are responsible for filing and paying Federal estimated quarterly taxes. They should also be paying estimated tax in states having a state income tax. This can be very different from the taxation that takes place while you are employed.

The term 'estimated quarterly taxes' isn't exactly accurate. The Internal Revenue Service publishes a schedule that jumps around a little. The first payment for a tax year is due April 15, the second payment is due June 15, the third payment is due October 15 and the last payment is due January 15 of the next year. So the payment schedule is more like three and a half months, two months, three months, and four months between Federal estimated quarterly tax payments. The intent is that each payment represents one quarter of what you will owe for the year.

It takes discipline to plan and set aside funds for tax payments throughout the year. If sufficient funds are not set aside as income is earned, then the individual or married couple will be put in a situation where some assets might have to be liquidated in order to come up with enough money to pay the taxes.

An easier method is for the individual or married couple to know what their approximate federal and state tax rates are and to apply those rates to income as it is earned. The calculated taxes should be set aside in a separate interest-bearing account until it is time to pay the estimated tax payments.

The IRS allows for two basic methods of calculating estimated taxes. An individual or married couple (if filing jointly) can elect to pay either:

1. An amount based on the total taxes paid in the previous year; or
2. At least ninety percent of the estimated taxes that will be due in the current year.

Remember, in either situation, the amounts paid are only for estimated taxes. The actual tax due will probably differ from the total of estimated taxes paid. If you elect to pay based on the prior year, the IRS allows you to calculate your amount and then spread that amount into four equal payments, paying them on the estimated tax due dates. The unrealistic assumption is that your income is consistent each month during the year. The payments can easily vary depending on your income.

**EXAMPLE:**
A married couple filed a joint return last year with total income of $160,000. The IRS formula is 100% of the prior year income if the income is less than $150,000 or 110% if greater than $150,000. If the couple paid Federal taxes of $42,000 last year on income of $160,000, this year's estimated taxes would be $42,000 X 1.10=$46,200. The estimated quarterly tax payments would be $11,550 due on each estimated tax installment date. Our software automatically makes this calculation when we

prepare the return and prints the necessary coupons for you with the amounts based on this method. If the individual elects to pay at least ninety percent of the estimated tax due during the current year, then the individual or married couple must keep track of income received during the year and make sure the total estimated taxes paid by the time the last installment is paid equals ninety percent of the actual tax that will be due at filing time. (This should be easy to do, even if the first three installments were insufficient, as the last installment date is January of the next calendar year. This allows you to adjust the last payment for any unexpected income.) The simplest approach is to look at two numbers on last year's tax return. On the 1040, divide the total tax on line 63 by the total income on line 22. The result is your effective tax rate. This is the percent you need to set aside for estimated taxes from all of your income during the year.

Failure to pay at least ninety percent of the tax due will result in a penalty being assessed on the amount failing to meet the ninety percent level. Keep in mind; the ninety percent option is just that; ninety percent of the actual tax that will be due by the April 15 filing date. If your payments just meet ninety percent of your taxes due, then the remaining ten percent will have to be paid by April 15.
One surprise people discover when choosing the ninety percent option is that at the time the first payment is due in the next year coincides with the annual filing from the last year. Thus, not only is the estimated quarterly payment due for the current year, but any remaining balance owed from the prior year, such as the ten percent not paid. If funds were not set aside, coming up with the monies to pay these taxes can be challenging.

Keep in mind; these rules apply to both federal and state taxes if your state has an income tax. In most states, the estimated taxes piggyback on the federal tax calculations.

**Tax Tip:** *Filing an extension only extends until October 15 the deadline for filing the return. Any tax due must be paid by April 15 to avoid a failure to pay penalty.*

**Tax Tip:** *There are two penalties involving payments that you want to avoid. One is the failure to pay any tax due by April 15. The second is what we are discussing above: the failure to pay, or not paying enough, estimated tax. These deposits must be made by Jan 15 for the prior year in order to avoid this penalty.*

# Strategy Eleven

*"If you want to know what God thinks of money just look at the people he gave it to."*

Dorothy Parker

# Give yourself a raise

If you or your spouse works at a W-2 job, here's an excellent way to give yourself a raise.

Remember, "Withholding" from your paycheck is a way to pre-pay your income taxes. Ideally, the amount withheld each year would total exactly what you owe in taxes. If you noted the correct number of allowances on the W-4 you filled out for your employer, then at the end of the year you wouldn't owe any additional taxes, and you wouldn't get a tax refund. It would be a wash.

Contrary to popular opinion, a refund is not a good thing. It simply means you "over withheld" for the previous year and now it's being returned. It means you gave Uncle Sam an interest-free loan of your money.

If you're starting a home-based business that qualifies you for additional deductions, you will be paying fewer taxes in the future. The amount you with hold on your W-2 paycheck can go down. Or, if you are accustomed to receiving large refunds, you also qualify to reduce your withholding. Either way, reducing the amount you withhold increases your take-home pay, which feels like a raise! An experienced tax advisor can help project how much your taxes may decrease.

Your next step is to fill out a new W-4, claiming the appropriate number of allowances, and submit it to your employer. If you increase your allowances, your take home pay will also increase.

The home-business tax deductions explained in this book will allow many people to claim additional allowances, which qualifies them to automatically increase the take home pay on their W-2 paychecks.

*So give yourself a raise!*

# Ignite Your Home Business Record Keeping System

**Ignite Your Finances Home Business Record Keeping System** designed by direct sellers for direct sellers. You talked and we listened. Rhonda designed all of our products to meet the needs of busy direct sellers' intent on building their business, increase their income, and spend more time with their families. After all, isn't that why you got into the "business" in the first place?

All of our products and designed to help you achieve your goals by minimizing the time you spend dealing with records...receipts, checkbooks, credit card statements. Maximize your time building the business. After all you didn't start a business to be a bookkeeper...you have a product or service that you are passionate about?

If you will spend a little time every month using the system, then by January of next year your reports summarizing your business for the year are ready to submit to your tax preparer. You will also have a month to month snapshot of just how profitable your business is as the year progresses.

You need this information in order to make intelligent decisions about your business. Maybe you need to emphasize different products, switch product lines, and get a different lead source or any number of other decisions that can be made much more intelligently if you have the facts on which to base your decisions.

More than 70% of Americans today are living paycheck to paycheck. "Track you're spending" is the #1 recommendation made by financial experts as a first step to getting out of debt. The Expense Tracker™ is the leader in providing a real-time, simple voice automated way to budget and find every penny. Featured on ABC, Fox Business News, Good Morning America, ZDNet, and ESPN, The Expense Tracker is at the core of the Ignite Your Finances Kit.

In addition to helping put your finances in order, this kit contains a suite of tools to help legitimize and grow your business, so that you can fully employ all of the business tax deductions and save even more starting from day one!

Other financial and tax systems online sell for well over $600 and they only give you part of what is offered here. With Ignite Your Finances Kit you not only get financial tracking to put your finances in order, but the tax information to help you business grow and even audit protection just in case. This is a must for anyone serious about growing their business.

# Ignite Your Finances ™
## Business In A Box Record Keeping System

These products were designed by direct sellers to help minimize the time spent keeping adequate records in order to help you maximize your deductions, and minimize your taxes so you keep more of what you make.

### *Making Tax A Game..."The Book"*

- A concise, easy to read (and understand) presentation of all the pertinent tax
  Laws relating to small and home-based business
- Let's learn the rules and play the game to win

*Mileage Log*...You Get Two...One For Each Vehicle

- Designed to meet IRS auto mileage log rules
- Simple spiral bound design
- Opens "flat" so it's easy to write on
- Keep it in your vehicle
- Fits in your glove box

*Tote Box*

- A simple satchel to store all of you tax documents for a year
- 6 File folder dividers to accumulate your business receipts
- Color coordinated with detailed instructions printed on the folders to remind
  you which receipts to put in each folder
- Accumulate all of the documents needed to prepare your taxes
- Send this Tote Box to your tax preparer at year end

*Making Tax A Game...Software*

- Simplest bookkeeping software ever
- Writ by direct sellers for direct sellers
- Easy to understand—no learning curve
- Intuitive and user friendly
- Record all your income and expenses
- Prints a comprehensive detailed or summary report over any date range
- You can edit the income and expense categories
- The yearend report will provide your tax preparer everything they need
  to prepare your return

### *The Trip Keeper*...Packet of (6)

- Stuff these convenient envelopes with all your travel receipts
- Use one for each business trip
- Record all your cash tips along with your credit card receipts
- Total them by category and store them with your travel receipts at home
- Save your convention badges, agenda, name tags to prove you were on a legitimate business trip

### *Receipt Tamer / Biz Tracker*

- Keep this handy little spiral bound, 4" square diary in your purse, glove box, or desk
- Each right-facing page has either a little stick dot to "hold" receipts or a slot to insert business cards
- You can make notes on the facing page, such as prospects, contacts, etc.
- Who, what, when, where you have business meals

### *Tax Savings Estimator*

- Calculate the approximate monthly tax savings your prospect is missing by not having a home based business
- Convenient tear-off pads to give your prospect
- One Tear Pad of Estimators in the kit
- Check out the phone app version at **http://taxapp.mobi**
- See a sample form on the next page...

### *Ignite Your Finances Planner*

- Day Timer / Planning Calendar
- Business Plan…just fill in the blanks
- Sheets for Notes
- Samples of **Trip Keeper** envelopes
- Slot for **Tax Savings Estimator** tear off pad

### *More Money Less Tax Prospecting Brochures*…Packet of (25)

- Rhonda & Tom outline the tax benefits of a home business
- And show your prospect how to get a raise at work by updating their W4
- Now they have the money needed to start a new business

All of these exciting record-keeping products designed by direct sellers for direct sellers are available at: **http://makingtaxagame.com**

# Tax Savings Estimator

Whether you already have a home-based business, or you are thinking of starting one, our Home Business Tax Savings Estimator will give you a good idea on how much you will save on taxes each year. After you calculate your annual savings, divide this number by 12 and this is your estimated amount of monthly income you could be getting back in your pocket starting with your very next paycheck. This is income you can use to start and build your home-based business!

These are just eight out of hundreds of possible deductions you could be receiving from your home-based business. Make sure to get the The 100% Home Business Tax Solution system today so you can start bringing home more money.

Fill out all the following information and see your tax savings grow as you fill in each field.

**Survey Questions**

| Survey Questions | | Deduction |
|---|---|---|
| 1. **Number of miles you drive each year** – include all cars (remember as a home-based business owner, a large part of your miles driven will be business miles): | 16543 | $8436.93 |
| 2. **Total vacation expenses for the year** (airfare, hotel, parking and other related business expenses): | $4752.00 | $4752.00 |
| 3. **Total cost of eating out** at breakfast, lunch and dinner for the year: | $2451.00 | $1225.50 |
| 4. **Annual cost of office supplies** (paper, ink, postage, envelopes, copies, etc.): | $587.00 | $587.00 |
| 5. **Annual cost of business items** (computers, printers, iPads, Androids, etc.): | $853.00 | $853.00 |
| 6. **Annual cost of marketing materials** (advertising, print, radio, tools, internet and other forms of marketing): | $1155.00 | $1155.00 |
| 7. **Annual cell phone expenses:** | $966.00 | $966.00 |
| 8. **Annual Internet access fee:** | $350.00 | $350.00 |
| Your total deductions | | **$18325.43** |
| 9. Select Your Tax Bracket | 25% | |
| Your estimated tax savings | | **$4581.36** |

# Form W-4 (2012)

**Purpose.** Complete Form W-4 so that your employer can withhold the correct federal income tax from your pay. Consider completing a new Form W-4 each year and when your personal or financial situation changes.

**Exemption from withholding.** If you are exempt, complete **only** lines 1, 2, 3, 4, and 7 and sign the form to validate it. Your exemption for 2012 expires February 18, 2013. See Pub. 505, Tax Withholding and Estimated Tax.

**Note.** If another person can claim you as a dependent on his or her tax return, you cannot claim exemption from withholding if your income exceeds $950 and includes more than $300 of unearned income (for example, interest and dividends).

**Basic instructions.** If you are not exempt, complete the **Personal Allowances Worksheet** below. The worksheets on page 2 further adjust your withholding allowances based on itemized deductions, certain credits, adjustments to income, or two-earners/multiple jobs situations.

Complete all worksheets that apply. However, you may claim fewer (or zero) allowances. For regular wages, withholding must be based on allowances you claimed and may not be a flat amount or percentage of wages.

**Head of household.** Generally, you can claim head of household filing status on your tax return only if you are unmarried and pay more than 50% of the costs of keeping up a home for yourself and your dependent(s) or other qualifying individuals. See Pub. 501, Exemptions, Standard Deduction, and Filing information, for information.

**Tax credits.** You can take projected tax credits into account in figuring your allowable number of withholding allowances. Credits for child or dependent care expenses and the child tax credit may be claimed using the **Personal Allowances Worksheet** below. See Pub. 505 for information on converting your other credits into withholding allowances.

**Nonwage income.** If you have a large amount of nonwage income, such as interest or dividends, consider making estimated tax payments using Form 1040-ES, Estimated Tax for Individuals. Otherwise, you may owe additional tax. If you have pension or annuity income, see Pub. 505 to find out if you should adjust your withholding on Form W-4 or W-4P.

**Two earners or multiple jobs.** If you have a working spouse or more than one job, figure the total number of allowances you are entitled to claim on all jobs using worksheets from only one Form W-4. Your withholding usually will be most accurate when all allowances are claimed on the Form W-4 for the highest paying job and zero allowances are claimed on the others. See Pub. 505 for details.

**Nonresident alien.** If you are a nonresident alien, see Notice 1392, Supplemental Form W-4 Instructions for Nonresident Aliens, before completing this form.

**Check your withholding.** After your Form W-4 takes effect, use Pub. 505 to see how the amount you are having withheld compares to your projected total tax for 2012. See Pub. 505, especially if your earnings exceed $130,000 (Single) or $180,000 (Married).

**Future developments.** The IRS has created a page on IRS.gov for information about Form W-4, at www.irs.gov/w4. Information about any future developments affecting Form W-4 (such as legislation enacted after we release it) will be posted on that page.

---

## Personal Allowances Worksheet (Keep for your records.)

A  Enter "1" for **yourself** if no one else can claim you as a dependent . . . . . . . . . . . . . . . . A _____

B  Enter "1" if:
- You are single and have only one job; or
- You are married, have only one job, and your spouse does not work; or
- Your wages from a second job or your spouse's wages (or the total of both) are $1,500 or less. . . . B _____

C  Enter "1" for your **spouse**. But, you may choose to enter "-0-" if you are married and have either a working spouse or more than one job. (Entering "-0-" may help you avoid having too little tax withheld.) . . . . . . . . . . . C _____

D  Enter number of **dependents** (other than your spouse or yourself) you will claim on your tax return . . . . . . D _____

E  Enter "1" if you will file **as head of household** on your tax return (see conditions under **Head of household** above) . . E _____

F  Enter "1" if you have at least $1,900 of **child or dependent care expenses** for which you plan to claim a credit . . . F _____
(**Note.** Do **not** include child support payments. See Pub. 503, Child and Dependent Care Expenses, for details.)

G  **Child Tax Credit** (including additional child tax credit). See Pub. 972, Child Tax Credit, for more information.
- If your total income will be less than $61,000 ($90,000 if married), enter "2" for each eligible child; then **less** "1" if you have three to seven eligible children or **less** "2" if you have eight or more eligible children.
- If your total income will be between $61,000 and $84,000 ($90,000 and $119,000 if married), enter "1" for each eligible child . . . G _____

H  Add lines A through G and enter total here. (**Note.** This may be different from the number of exemptions you claim on your tax return.) ▶ H _____

For accuracy, complete all worksheets that apply.
- If you plan to **itemize** or claim adjustments to income and want to reduce your withholding, see the **Deductions and Adjustments Worksheet** on page 2.
- If you are **single and have more than one job** or are **married and you and your spouse both work** and the combined earnings from all jobs exceed $40,000 ($10,000 if married), see the **Two-Earners/Multiple Jobs Worksheet** on page 2 to avoid having too little tax withheld.
- If **neither** of the above situations applies, **stop here** and enter the number from line H on line 5 of Form W-4 below.

--------- Separate here and give Form W-4 to your employer. Keep the top part for your records. ---------

---

Form **W-4**
Department of the Treasury
Internal Revenue Service

## Employee's Withholding Allowance Certificate

OMB No. 1545-0074

**2012**

▶ Whether you are entitled to claim a certain number of allowances or exemption from withholding is subject to review by the IRS. Your employer may be required to send a copy of this form to the IRS.

| 1 Your first name and middle initial | Last name | | 2 Your social security number |
|---|---|---|---|

Home address (number and street or rural route)

City or town, state, and ZIP code

3 ☐ Single  ☐ Married  ☐ Married, but withhold at higher Single rate.
**Note.** If married, but legally separated, or spouse is a nonresident alien, check the "Single" box.

4 If your last name differs from that shown on your social security card, check here. You must call 1-800-772-1213 for a replacement card. ▶ ☐

5  Total number of allowances you are claiming (from line **H** above **or** from the applicable worksheet on page 2)  5 _____

6  Additional amount, if any, you want withheld from each paycheck . . . . . . . . . . . . . . . 6 $ _____

7  I claim exemption from withholding for 2012, and I certify that I meet **both** of the following conditions for exemption.
- Last year I had a right to a refund of **all** federal income tax withheld because I had **no** tax liability, **and**
- This year I expect a refund of **all** federal income tax withheld because I expect to have **no** tax liability.
If you meet both conditions, write "Exempt" here . . . . . . . . . . . . ▶ 7 _____

Under penalties of perjury, I declare that I have examined this certificate and, to the best of my knowledge and belief, it is true, correct, and complete.

**Employee's signature**
(This form is not valid unless you sign it.) ▶                                          Date ▶

| 8 Employer's name and address (Employer: Complete lines 8 and 10 only if sending to the IRS.) | 9 Office code (optional) | 10 Employer identification number (EIN) |
|---|---|---|

For Privacy Act and Paperwork Reduction Act Notice, see page 2.      Cat. No. 10220Q      Form **W-4** (2012)

Form **1040**  Department of the Treasury — Internal Revenue Service  **U.S. Individual Income Tax Return** **2009** (99) IRS Use Only — Do not write or staple in this space.

For the year Jan 1 - Dec 31, 2009, or other tax year beginning , 2009, ending , 20    OMB No. 1545-0074

| **Label** (See instructions.) | Your first name | MI | Last name | | Your social security number |
|---|---|---|---|---|---|
| | George | | Clooney | | 538-55-1234 |
| **Use the IRS label.** | If a joint return, spouse's first name | MI | Last name | | Spouse's social security number |
| | Rhonda | | Clooney | | 544-33-1234 |

**Otherwise, please print or type.**

Home address (number and street). If you have a P.O. box, see instructions.  Apartment no.

13334 NE 99th Place

City, town or post office. If you have a foreign address, see instructions.  State  ZIP code

Redmond, WA 98021

You **must** enter your social security number(s) above. ▲

**Presidential Election Campaign**

Checking a box below will not change your tax or refund.

► Check here if you, or your spouse if filing jointly, want $3 to go to this fund? (see instructions) ............ ► ☐ You  ☐ Spouse

**Filing Status**

Check only one box.

1 ☐ Single
2 ☒ Married filing jointly (even if only one had income)
3 ☐ Married filing separately. Enter spouse's SSN above & full name here. ►
4 ☐ Head of household (with qualifying person). (See instructions.) If the qualifying person is a child but not your dependent, enter this child's name here. ►
5 ☐ Qualifying widow(er) with dependent child (see instructions)

**Exemptions**

6a ☒ Yourself. If someone can claim you as a dependent, do **not** check box 6a ............
b ☒ Spouse ..................................................................

Boxes checked on 6a and 6b ............ **2**

No. of children on 6c who:

| c Dependents: | (2) Dependent's social security number | (3) Dependent's relationship to you | (4) ✓ if qualifying child for child tax credit (see instrs) |
|---|---|---|---|
| (1) First name   Last name | | | |
| Morgan Clooney | 534-45-1234 | Daughter | ☒ |
| Jack Clooney | 455-12-5431 | Son | ☒ |

• lived with you ..... **2**
• did not live with you due to divorce or separation (see instrs). ....
Dependents on 6c not entered above ....

If more than four dependents, see instructions and check here ► ☐

d Total number of exemptions claimed ......................................... Add numbers on lines above ► **4**

**Income**

**Attach Form(s) W-2 here. Also attach Forms W-2G and 1099-R if tax was withheld.**

**If you did not get a W-2, see instructions.**

**Enclose, but do not attach, any payment. Also, please use Form 1040-V.**

| | | | |
|---|---|---|---|
| 7 | Wages, salaries, tips, etc. Attach Form(s) W-2 .......................... | 7 | 96,725. |
| 8a | Taxable interest. Attach Schedule B if required ......................... | 8a | 32. |
| b | Tax-exempt interest. Do **not** include on line 8a ...... | 8b | | |
| 9a | Ordinary dividends. Attach Schedule B if required ...................... | 9a | |
| b | Qualified dividends (see instrs) ...... | 9b | | |
| 10 | Taxable refunds, credits, or offsets of state and local income taxes (see instructions) | 10 | |
| 11 | Alimony received ................................................ | 11 | |
| 12 | Business income or (loss). Attach Schedule C or C-EZ .................. | 12 | |
| 13 | Capital gain or (loss). Att Sch D if reqd. If not reqd, ck here ...... ► ☐ | 13 | |
| 14 | Other gains or (losses). Attach Form 4797 ............................ | 14 | |
| 15a | IRA distributions ...... | 15a | b Taxable amount (see instrs) . | 15b | |
| 16a | Pensions and annuities ...... | 16a | b Taxable amount (see instrs) . | 16b | |
| 17 | Rental real estate, royalties, partnerships, S corporations, trusts, etc. Attach Schedule E . | 17 | |
| 18 | Farm income or (loss). Attach Schedule F .............................. | 18 | |
| 19 | Unemployment compensation in excess of $2,400 for recipient (see instructions). | 19 | 2,480. |
| 20a | Social security benefits ...... | 20a | b Taxable amount (see instrs) . | 20b | |
| 21 | Other income | 21 | |
| 22 | Add the amounts in the far right column for lines 7 through 21. This is your **total income** ..... ► | 22 | 99,237. |

**Adjusted Gross Income**

| | | | |
|---|---|---|---|
| 23 | Educator expenses (see instructions) ........ | 23 | |
| 24 | Certain business expenses of reservists, performing artists, and fee-basis government officials. Attach Form 2106 or 2106-EZ .......... | 24 | |
| 25 | Health savings account deduction. Attach Form 8889 ...... | 25 | |
| 26 | Moving expenses. Attach Form 3903 ............ | 26 | |
| 27 | One-half of self-employment tax. Attach Schedule SE ...... | 27 | |
| 28 | Self-employed SEP, SIMPLE, and qualified plans .......... | 28 | |
| 29 | Self-employed health insurance deduction (see instructions) ............ | 29 | |
| 30 | Penalty on early withdrawal of savings ...................... | 30 | |
| 31 a | Alimony paid  b Recipient's SSN ... ► | 31 a | |
| 32 | IRA deduction (see instructions) ................ | 32 | |
| 33 | Student loan interest deduction (see instructions) ............ | 33 | |
| 34 | Tuition and fees deduction. Attach Form 8917 ...... | 34 | |
| 35 | Domestic production activities deduction. Attach Form 8903 ...... | 35 | |
| 36 | Add lines 23 - 31a and 32 - 35 ............................ | 36 | 0. |
| 37 | Subtract line 36 from line 22. This is your **adjusted gross income** ............ ► | 37 | 99,237. |

**BAA For Disclosure, Privacy Act, and Paperwork Reduction Act Notice, see instructions.**  FDIA0112L 09/17/09  Form **1040** (2009)

George and Rhonda Clooney  538-55-1234

| | | | |
|---|---|---|---|
| **Tax and Credits** | 38 Amount from line 37 (adjusted gross income) | **38** | 55,859. |

**Standard Deduction for –**
- People who check any box on line 39a, 39b, or 40b or who can be claimed as a dependent, see instructions.
- All others:

Single or Married filing separately, $5,700

Married filing jointly or Qualifying widow(er), $11,400

Head of household, $8,350

| | | |
|---|---|---|
| 39a Check if: | You were born before January 2, 1945, ☐  Blind. **Total boxes** Spouse was born before January 2, 1945, ☐  Blind. **checked** ► 39a ☐ | |
| b | If your spouse itemizes on a separate return, or you were a dual-status alien, see instrs and ck here ► 39b ☐ | |
| 40a | Itemized deductions (from Schedule A) or your standard deduction (see left margin) | 40a | 22,581. |
| b | If you are increasing your standard deduction by certain real estate taxes, new motor vehicle taxes, or a net disaster loss, attach Schedule L and check here (see instructions) ► 40b ☐ | |
| 41 | Subtract line 40a from line 38 | 41 | 33,278. |
| 42 | Exemptions. If line 38 is $125,100 or less and you did not provide housing to a Midwestern displaced individual, multiply $3,650 by the number on line 6d. Otherwise, see instructions | 42 | 14,600. |
| 43 | Taxable income. Subtract line 42 from line 41. If line 42 is more than line 41, enter -0- | 43 | 18,678. |
| 44 | **Tax** (see instrs). Check if any tax is from: a ☐ Form(s) 8814 b ☐ Form 4972 | 44 | 1,966. |
| 45 | **Alternative minimum tax** (see instructions). Attach Form 6251 | 45 | 0. |
| 46 | Add lines 44 and 45 ► | 46 | 1,966. |
| 47 | Foreign tax credit. Attach Form 1116 if required | 47 | |
| 48 | Credit for child and dependent care expenses. Attach Form 2441 | 48 | |
| 49 | Education credits from Form 8863, line 29 | 49 | |
| 50 | Retirement savings contributions credit. Attach Form 8880 | 50 | |
| 51 | Child tax credit (see instructions) | 51 1,966. | |
| 52 | Credits from Form: a ☐ 8396 b ☐ 8839 c ☐ 5695 | 52 | |
| 53 | Other crs from Form: a ☐ 3800 b ☐ 8801 c ☐ | 53 | |
| 54 | Add lines 47 through 53. These are your **total credits** | 54 | 1,966. |
| 55 | Subtract line 54 from line 46. If line 54 is more than line 46, enter -0- ► | 55 | 0. |

| | | | |
|---|---|---|---|
| **Other Taxes** | 56 Self-employment tax. Attach Schedule SE | **56** | |
| | 57 Unreported social security and Medicare tax from Form: a ☐ 4137 b ☐ 8919 | 57 | |
| | 58 Additional tax on IRAs, other qualified retirement plans, etc. Attach Form 5329 if required | 58 | |
| | 59 Additional taxes: a ☐ AEIC payments  b ☐ Household employment taxes. Attach Schedule H | 59 | |
| | 60 Add lines 55-59. This is your **total tax** ► | 60 | 0. |

| | | | |
|---|---|---|---|
| **Payments** | 61 Federal income tax withheld from Forms W-2 and 1099 | 61 6,480. | |
| | 62 2009 estimated tax payments and amount applied from 2008 return | 62 | |
| If you have a qualifying child, attach Schedule EIC. | 63 Making work pay and government retiree credit. Attach Schedule M | 63 800. | |
| | 64a **Earned income credit (EIC)** | 64a | |
| | b Nontaxable combat pay election ► 64b | | |
| | 65 Additional child tax credit. Attach Form 8812 | 65 34. | |
| | 66 Refundable education credit from Form 8863, line 16 | 66 | |
| | 67 First-time homebuyer credit. Attach Form 5405 | 67 | |
| | 68 Amount paid with request for extension to file (see instructions) | 68 | |
| | 69 Excess social security and tier 1 RRTA tax withheld (see instructions) | 69 | |
| | 70 Credits from Form: a ☐ 2439 b ☐ 4136 c ☐ 8801 d ☐ 8885 | 70 | |
| | 71 Add lns 61-63, 64a, & 65-70. These are your **total pmts** ► | **71** | 7,314. |

| | | | |
|---|---|---|---|
| **Refund** | 72 If line 71 is more than line 60, subtract line 60 from line 71. This is the amount you **overpaid** | **72** | 7,314. |
| Direct deposit? See instructions and fill in 73b, 73c, and 73d or Form 8888. | 73a Amount of line 72 you want **refunded to you**. If Form 8888 is attached, check here ► ☐ | 73a | 7,314. |
| | ► b Routing number XXXXXXXXX  ► c Type: ☐ Checking ☐ Savings | | |
| | ► d Account number XXXXXXXXXXXXXXXXX | | |
| | 74 Amount of line 72 you want applied to your 2010 estimated tax ► 74 | | |

| | | | |
|---|---|---|---|
| **Amount You Owe** | 75 **Amount you owe.** Subtract line 71 from line 60. For details on how to pay, see instructions ► | **75** | |
| | 76 Estimated tax penalty (see instructions) | 76 | |

| | |
|---|---|
| **Third Party Designee** | Do you want to allow another person to discuss this return with the IRS (see instructions)? ☐ **Yes. Complete the following.** ☒ **No** Designee's name ►   Phone no. ►   Personal identification number (PIN) ► |

**Sign Here**
Joint return? See instructions.
Keep a copy for your records.

Under penalties of perjury, I declare that I have examined this return and accompanying schedules and statements, and to the best of my knowledge and belief, they are true, correct, and complete. Declaration of preparer (other than taxpayer) is based on all information of which preparer has any knowledge.

| Your signature | Date | Your occupation  Actor | Daytime phone number |
|---|---|---|---|
| Spouse's signature. If a joint return, both must sign. | Date | Spouse's occupation  Trophy Wife | |

| | | | |
|---|---|---|---|
| **Paid Preparer's Use Only** | Preparer's signature ► Self-Prepared | Date | Check if self-employed ☐ | Preparer's SSN or PTIN |
| | Firm's name (or yours if self-employed), address, and ZIP code ► | | EIN  Phone no. |

Form **1040** (2009)

FDIA0112L  09/17/09

162

Form **1040**  Department of the Treasury — Internal Revenue Service
**U.S. Individual Income Tax Return** **2009** (99) IRS Use Only — Do not write or staple in this space.

For the year Jan 1 - Dec 31, 2009, or other tax year beginning , 2009, ending , 20    OMB No. 1545-0074

**Label** (See instructions.)

| | | |
|---|---|---|
| Your first name MI Last name | | Your social security number |
| George Clooney | | 538-55-1234 |

**Use the IRS label.**

| | | |
|---|---|---|
| If a joint return, spouse's first name MI Last name | | Spouse's social security number |
| Rhonda Clooney | | 544-33-1234 |

**Otherwise, please print or type.**

Home address (number and street). If you have a P.O. box, see instructions.    Apartment no.
13334 NE 99th Place

You **must** enter your social security number(s) above. ▲

City, town or post office. If you have a foreign address, see instructions.    State   ZIP code
Redmond, WA 98021

Checking a box below will not change your tax or refund.

**Presidential Election Campaign**
► Check here if you, or your spouse if filing jointly, want $3 to go to this fund? (see instructions)............ ► ☐ You  ☐ Spouse

**Filing Status**

Check only one box.

1 ☐ Single
2 ☒ Married filing jointly (even if only one had income)
3 ☐ Married filing separately. Enter spouse's SSN above & full name here. ►
4 ☐ Head of household (with qualifying person). (See instructions.) If the qualifying person is a child but not your dependent, enter this child's name here ►
5 ☐ Qualifying widow(er) with dependent child (see instructions)

**Exemptions**

6a ☒ Yourself. If someone can claim you as a dependent, **do not** check box 6a............
b ☒ Spouse........................................................................

Boxes checked on 6a and 6b ... **2**

| c Dependents: | (2) Dependent's social security number | (3) Dependent's relationship to you | (4)✓ if qualifying child for child tax credit (see instrs) |
|---|---|---|---|
| (1) First name    Last name | | | |
| Morgan Clooney | 534-45-1234 | Daughter | ☒ |
| Jack Clooney | 455-12-5431 | Son | ☒ |
| | | | |
| | | | |

If more than four dependents, see instructions and check here ► ☐

No. of children on 6c who:
● lived with you ...... **2**
● did not live with you due to divorce or separation (see instrs) ...
Dependents on 6c not entered above ...
Add numbers on lines above ► **4**

d Total number of exemptions claimed.................................................

**Income**

Attach Form(s) W-2 here. Also attach Forms W-2G and 1099-R if tax was withheld.

If you did not get a W-2, see instructions.

Enclose, but do not attach, any payment. Also, please use Form 1040-V.

| | | |
|---|---|---|
| 7 Wages, salaries, tips, etc. Attach Form(s) W-2.................... | 7 | 70,023. |
| 8a Taxable interest. Attach Schedule B if required................. | 8a | 32. |
| b Tax-exempt interest. Do not include on line 8a........ 8b | | |
| 9a Ordinary dividends. Attach Schedule B if required............. | 9a | |
| b Qualified dividends (see instrs)................. 9b | | |
| 10 Taxable refunds, credits, or offsets of state and local income taxes (see instructions)... | 10 | |
| 11 Alimony received................................................ | 11 | |
| 12 Business income or (loss). Attach Schedule C or C-EZ........... | 12 | -16,676. |
| 13 Capital gain or (loss). Att Sch D if reqd. If not reqd, ck here...... ► ☐ | 13 | |
| 14 Other gains or (losses). Attach Form 4797.................... | 14 | |
| 15a IRA distributions........... 15a    b Taxable amount (see instrs). | 15b | |
| 16a Pensions and annuities..... 16a    b Taxable amount (see instrs). | 16b | |
| 17 Rental real estate, royalties, partnerships, S corporations, trusts, etc. Attach Schedule E. | 17 | |
| 18 Farm income or (loss). Attach Schedule F.................... | 18 | |
| 19 Unemployment compensation in excess of $2,400 per recipient (see instructions)... | 19 | 2,480. |
| 20a Social security benefits......... 20a    b Taxable amount (see instrs). | 20b | |
| 21 Other income...................................................... | 21 | |
| 22 Add the amounts in the far right column for lines 7 through 21. This is your **total income**..... ► | 22 | 55,859. |

**Adjusted Gross Income**

| | | |
|---|---|---|
| 23 Educator expenses (see instructions).............. 23 | | |
| 24 Certain business expenses of reservists, performing artists, and fee-basis government officials. Attach Form 2106 or 2106-EZ. 24 | | |
| 25 Health savings account deduction. Attach Form 8889. 25 | | |
| 26 Moving expenses. Attach Form 3903............ 26 | | |
| 27 One-half of self-employment tax. Attach Schedule SE ...... 27 | | |
| 28 Self-employed SEP, SIMPLE, and qualified plans......... 28 | | |
| 29 Self-employed health insurance deduction (see instructions).... 29 | | |
| 30 Penalty on early withdrawal of savings............... 30 | | |
| 31a Alimony paid b Recipient's SSN.... ► 31a | | |
| 32 IRA deduction (see instructions)................ 32 | | |
| 33 Student loan interest deduction (see instructions).......... 33 | | |
| 34 Tuition and fees deduction. Attach Form 8917............. 34 | | |
| 35 Domestic production activities deduction. Attach Form 8903 ... 35 | | |
| 36 Add lines 23 - 31a and 32 - 35.................... | 36 | 0. |
| 37 Subtract line 36 from line 22. This is your **adjusted gross income**..... ► | 37 | 55,859. |

BAA For Disclosure, Privacy Act, and Paperwork Reduction Act Notice, see instructions.    FDIA0112L  09/17/09    Form **1040** (2009)

| Tax and Credits | 38 | Amount from line 37 (adjusted gross income) | | | 38 | 99,237. |
|---|---|---|---|---|---|---|
| | 39a | Check if: ☐ You were born before January 2, 1945, ☐ Blind. **Total boxes** ☐ Spouse was born before January 2, 1945, ☐ Blind. **checked** ► 39a | | | | |
| **Standard Deduction for —** | b | If your spouse itemizes on a separate return, or you were a dual-status alien, see instrs and ck here ► 39b ☐ | | | | |
| • People who check any box on line 39a, 39b, or 40b or who can be claimed as a dependent, see instructions. | 40a | Itemized deductions (from Schedule A) or your standard deduction (see left margin) | | | 40a | 23,532. |
| | b | If you are increasing your standard deduction by certain real estate taxes, new motor vehicle taxes, or a net disaster loss, attach Schedule L and check here (see instructions) ► 40b ☐ | | | | |
| | 41 | Subtract line 40a from line 38 | | | 41 | 75,705. |
| | 42 | Exemptions. If line 38 is $125,100 or less and you did not provide housing to a Midwestern displaced individual, multiply $3,650 by the number on line 6d. Otherwise, see instructions | | | 42 | 14,600. |
| • All others: | 43 | Taxable income. Subtract line 42 from line 41. If line 42 is more than line 41, enter -0- | | | 43 | 61,105. |
| Single or Married filing separately, $5,700 | 44 | Tax (see instrs). Check if any tax is from: a ☐ Form(s) 8814 b ☐ Form 4972 | | | 44 | 8,334. |
| | 45 | Alternative minimum tax (see instructions). Attach Form 6251 | | | 45 | 0. |
| Married filing jointly or Qualifying widow(er), $11,400 | 46 | Add lines 44 and 45 | | ► | 46 | 8,334. |
| | 47 | Foreign tax credit. Attach Form 1116 if required | 47 | | | |
| | 48 | Credit for child and dependent care expenses. Attach Form 2441 | 48 | | | |
| Head of household, $8,350 | 49 | Education credits from Form 8863, line 29 | 49 | | | |
| | 50 | Retirement savings contributions credit. Attach Form 8880 | 50 | | | |
| | 51 | Child tax credit (see instructions) | 51 | 2,000. | | |
| | 52 | Credits from Form: a ☐ 8396 b ☐ 8839 c ☐ 5695 | 52 | | | |
| | 53 | Other crs from Form: a ☐ 3800 b ☐ 8801 c ☐ | 53 | | | |
| | 54 | Add lines 47 through 53. These are your total credits | | | 54 | 2,000. |
| | 55 | Subtract line 54 from line 46. If line 54 is more than line 46, enter -0- | | ► | 55 | 6,334. |
| **Other Taxes** | 56 | Self-employment tax. Attach Schedule SE | | | 56 | |
| | 57 | Unreported social security and Medicare tax from Form: a ☐ 4137 b ☐ 8919 | | | 57 | |
| | 58 | Additional tax on IRAs, other qualified retirement plans, etc. Attach Form 5329 if required | | | 58 | |
| | 59 | Additional taxes: a ☐ AEIC payments b ☐ Household employment taxes. Attach Schedule H | | | 59 | |
| | 60 | Add lines 55-59. This is your total tax | | | 60 | 6,334. |
| **Payments** | 61 | Federal income tax withheld from Forms W-2 and 1099 | 61 | 6,480. | | |
| | 62 | 2009 estimated tax payments and amount applied from 2008 return | 62 | | | |
| If you have a qualifying child, attach Schedule EIC. | 63 | Making work pay and government retiree credit. Attach Schedule M | 63 | 800. | | |
| | 64a | Earned income credit (EIC) | 64a | | | |
| | b | Nontaxable combat pay election ► 64b | | | | |
| | 65 | Additional child tax credit. Attach Form 8812 | 65 | | | |
| | 66 | Refundable education credit from Form 8863, line 16 | 66 | | | |
| | 67 | First-time homebuyer credit. Attach Form 5405 | 67 | | | |
| | 68 | Amount paid with request for extension to file (see instructions) | 68 | | | |
| | 69 | Excess social security and tier 1 RRTA tax withheld (see instructions) | 69 | | | |
| | 70 | Credits from Form: a ☐ 2439 b ☐ 4136 c ☐ 8801 d ☐ 8885 | 70 | | | |
| | 71 | Add lns 61-63, 64a, & 65-70. These are your total pmts | | ► | 71 | 7,280. |
| **Refund** | 72 | If line 71 is more than line 60, subtract line 60 from line 71. This is the amount you overpaid | | | 72 | 946. |
| Direct deposit? See instructions and fill in 73b, 73c, and 73d or Form 8888. | 73a | Amount of line 72 you want refunded to you. If Form 8888 is attached, check here ► ☐ | | | 73a | 946. |
| | | ► b Routing number XXXXXXXXXX ► c Type: ☐ Checking ☐ Savings | | | | |
| | | ► d Account number XXXXXXXXXXXXXXXXXXXX | | | | |
| | 74 | Amount of line 72 you want applied to your 2010 estimated tax ► 74 | | | | |
| **Amount You Owe** | 75 | Amount you owe. Subtract line 71 from line 60. For details on how to pay, see instructions ► | | | 75 | |
| | 76 | Estimated tax penalty (see instructions) | 76 | | | |
| **Third Party Designee** | Do you want to allow another person to discuss this return with the IRS (see instructions)? ☐ Yes. Complete the following. ☒ No | | | | | |
| | Designee's name ► | Phone no. ► | | Personal identification number (PIN) ► | | |

**Sign Here**
Joint return? See instructions.
Keep a copy for your records.

Under penalties of perjury, I declare that I have examined this return and accompanying schedules and statements, and to the best of my knowledge and belief, they are true, correct, and complete. Declaration of preparer (other than taxpayer) is based on all information of which preparer has any knowledge.

| Your signature ► | Date | Your occupation Actor | Daytime phone number |
|---|---|---|---|
| Spouse's signature. If a joint return, both must sign. ► | Date | Spouse's occupation Trophy Wife | |

**Paid Preparer's Use Only**

| Preparer's signature ► Self-Prepared | Date | Check if self-employed ☐ | Preparer's SSN or PTIN |
|---|---|---|---|
| Firm's name (or yours if self-employed) address, and ZIP code ► | | EIN | |
| | | Phone no. | |

Form **1040** (2009)